Grasping Wastrels
vs.
Beaches Forever Inc.

Covering the Fights for the Soul of the Oregon Coast

Governor Tom McCall in front of the Surfsand Motel in Cannon Beach.

by Matt Love

Copyright 2003
Nestucca Spit Press
Pacific City, Oregon
ISBN: 0-9744364-0-2

First edition press run of 1000 copies

A harbor seal on Nestucca Spit with its head blown off.

For my mother and father

They taught me long ago: "...what men can't teach you at Lake Success."

Oregonians fishing for perch on Nestucca Spit.

Introduction

The term "Grasping Wastrels" comes from a 1973 speech to the Oregon Legislature by Governor Tom McCall. "The interests of Oregon for today and in the future must be protected from the grasping wastrels of the land," he said. If the Oregon Coast is a boxing ring, McCall's "Grasping Wastrels" are in one corner.

The second half of the title, "Beaches Forever Inc.," derives from a political organization formed in 1968 by State Treasurer Bob Straub to qualify and pass a ballot initiative that would have authorized and funded the purchase of undeveloped Oregon beachfront property from willing sellers. The initiative made the ballot but voters rejected it and Beaches Forever Inc. died. Fortunately, its holy conservation spirit resurrected in the 1970s and has since imbued thousands of Oregonians with a passion to protect their coastline. These Oregonians are in the other corner.

When the Grasping Wastrels and Beaches Forever Inc. go at it, they fight. At stake is the soul of the Oregon Coast. From what I can tell from my research and experience, these fights aren't fixed. Thus, they must be fought and that's why these pieces were originally written and now presented as a self-published book. It's my small way of fighting for the soul of the Oregon Coast.

I'm well into my sixth year on the Oregon Coast, in South Tillamook County, but many who have lived here longer consider me and other transplants from Portland as "outsiders." To them, our ideas are practically venereal. This is a very small opposition group, more like a cabal. They're atypical and loud. They're not representative. The vast majority of Tillamook County residents have welcomed me into the community and quietly modeled a special appreciation for their local natural world. They also taught me how to live a full life.

This cabal, well, it boasts some interesting members. It's especially interesting when one of them calls you late at night, delivers a barely lucid harangue, labels you an "outsider," repeatedly interjects the number "1601," (read on to uncover the mystery) and then hangs up! That kind of shit actually happens in Tillamook County, and is one reason why it makes it an occasionally interesting place to live and write about.

For the record, if you grew up in Oregon, which I did in Oregon City overlooking the Willamette Falls, or have lived in this state for any length of time, you're *never* an "outsider" to the Oregon Coast. Every Oregonian is a "local" when it comes to the Oregon Coast. Traveling to the beach on a whim, need for truancy, vision, bender, alone, with a crush date, with Whitman or Kerouac, or part of a family vacation, is what being an Oregonian is all about.

Booknotes

Many of these essays originally appeared, in some form or another, in the Astoria-based alternative monthly, *Hipfish*, as a monthly column called "Uncommontary."

I want to thank my great friend Cindy Popp for the cover art. I appreciate Sara Ogle's unflinching editorial advice. I received special encouragement from Super K. I designed the book and took all the photographs except the ones of Tom McCall, Samuel Boardman's car and Dr. Bacon.

I include a bibliography for those interested in my source material. I also drew upon the experience of attending well over 100 public meetings related to Oregon Coast environmental issues, interviews with many people, and driving up and down Highway 101 uncountable times in the course of my journalism and recreation. Moreover, since I live near the beach and visit almost every day, (and in fact have visited every county and state park on the Oregon Coast) many of the impressions and opinions presented in these essays are the direct result of hanging out there.

Please contact me at (bobcatsports@excite.com) regarding the book.

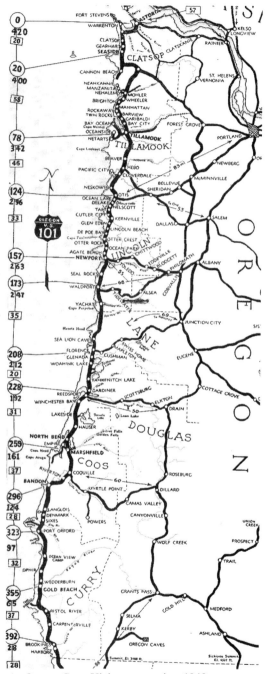

An Oregon Coast Highway map circa 1940.

Riprap on a stretch of Neskowin Beach.

Contents

A plaque In Oswald West State Park commemorating reporter Matt Kramer.

To me, and thousands of other Oregonians, the prospect of 'Private Beach—No Trespassing' signs was not just unacceptable, it was *unthinkable*.

Oregon Governor Bob Straub, 1977

The "No Camping" sign on Neahkahnie Beach.

Fine Americans Conceived

In 1913 Oregon Governor Oswald West signed a bill into law. The law declared the state's beaches a public highway and thus public property forever. When West affixed his signature he said: "No local selfish interest should be permitted, through politics or otherwise, to destroy or even impair this great birthright of our people."

In an ingeniously brief 66-word piece of legislation that he wrote, West saved Oregon from the blight and disgrace of privately owned beaches, something horrifying many Oregonians have witnessed in other states and countries. Earlier in 1913, long before Highway 101 pounded over the Oregon Coast's rugged headlands, Governor West rode horseback, solo, wearing a Stetson, on a mail trail from Cannon

1

Beach over Arch Cape and Neahkahnie Mountain into Nehalem. He claimed this experience inspired him to write the bill.

Governor West established an ideal. He established that Oregon viewed and would treat its beaches in a different way.

West's bill wouldn't even get a committee hearing today.

Back in 1914, Oregon voters refused West a second term. He ended up a lobbyist.

Years after his defeat, the state acquired part of the land he rode through on the North Coast and developed it into one of the finest state parks in the country, Short Sand Beach. In 1958 it was renamed Oswald West State Park. A plaque erected on site once read: "If sight of sand and sky and sea has given respite from your daily cares, then pause to thank Oswald West."

A few years after the renaming, locals petitioned the state to change the name back to Short Sand Beach. Apparently they felt Governor West no longer deserved the honor.

Today, there's no trace of the plaque. A wood sign that barely mentions West's contribution fell victim to a downed tree a few years ago. No one has bothered to re-erect the sign. It now collects mold in a storage shed.

Oswald West State Park is my favorite park in Oregon for many reasons:

—because as a seventh grader I made out there in the driftwood with an exotic ninth grader, Shelly, touching her black bra;

—because campers have to haul their gear down to the beach in a wheelbarrow;

—because it has old tall trees on the Oregon Coast that the Oregon Department of Forestry can't cut to improve nature;

—because the surfers give it a non-consumptive vibe;

—because there's an extraordinary plaque on the way to Falcon Cove thanking a reporter named Matt Kramer for his efforts to save Oregon's beaches. You can hear the waves pop behind as you read: "The people of Oregon hereby express their gratitude to Matt Kramer of the Associated Press, whose clear and incisive newspaper articles were instrumental in gaining public support for passing of the 1967 Beach Bill." I look at the plaque and it's all I wish for an Oregon writing life.

Fifty-four years after Governor West took his ride, another Oregon Governor took a ride.

In the summer of 1966 a Cannon Beach motel owner, William Hay, fenced off part of the beach in front of his property for the exclusive use of his guests and kicked off a couple having a picnic there. In effect, he privatized a section of beach. Hay's action constituted an unprecedented and vicious attack on West's ideal. He was practically giving the middle finger to the Oregon people. It quickly caught the attention of people who wanted to preserve the tradition of open Oregon beaches.

In January 1967 the Oregon Legislature convened and the State Highway Commission promoted a bill, House Bill 1601, to establish public ownership of the dry sands area that were ill defined by West's original law. The bill languished in the House Highway Committee dominated by rural Republicans. It was going nowhere and most certainly would have died unless the public spoke up. After some dogged and enlightening reporting by Kramer and a televised editorial warning about the threat to Oregon's beaches, the public did speak--by sending a record number of letters and telegrams.

This caught the attention of the state's new chief executive, Tom McCall. He decided to check things out by visiting the Oregon Coast by helicopter. One of those places was Cannon Beach, in front of Hay's motel.

Flanked by reporters and surveyors, wearing a dark sport coat, a dark turtleneck, dark loafers, dark glasses, hair slicked back, McCall marched alone up to the motel, stared at it for the still cameras, steamed, cussed out Hay, then boldly explained on camera the concept of public ownership of Oregon's beaches, access to these beaches, and the limitation on private property rights.

It was probably the first televised, coded middle finger to the developer class in American history. I consider McCall's act the finest moment in Oregon politics, an event that topped even West's wild, romantic ride. It said: "We're different." It blasted the bill out of the craven House Highway Committee and onto the floor where it passed 57-3 with the only "No" votes coming from coastal lawmakers. The Senate tweaked the bill a bit, approved it 27-0, then sent it back to House where it passed 36-20.

When McCall signed the bill into law, he quoted what

4

West said in 1913: "No local selfish interest should be permitted, through politics or otherwise, to destroy or even impair this great birthright of our people."

The Beach Bill wouldn't even get a committee hearing today.

Now over 35 years later, a small but symbolic drama over camping on a section of Neahkahnie Beach has played out. The end result is roughly metaphysically equal to disinterring West and McCall's remains to make way for a gated coastal subdivision or a golf course.

It reminded me that the struggle for control of Oregon's beaches is never over—as it should be—with every matter impacting beach access and development decided in favor of the most beneficial public use for *all* Oregonians.

These days when I walk Neahkahnie Beach and look north to the mountain West rode over (now covered by mansions), I imagine a reincarnated McCall landing in a helicopter, marching up to one of the weekend-a-month palaces at the heart of the controversy, pointing a finger, maybe a middle one, naming a name for the press, and flat out getting it on with some tycoon while the cameras roll.

That's a fantasy. Here's the reality:

In the spring of 2000, a few people who owned expensive property near Neahkahnie Beach (all occasional weekenders, year-round residents told me) complained to various government agencies about garbage (including human feces) left behind by overnighters and the threat of ill-managed campfires in the dunes burning down beachfront homes. They wanted the Oregon Parks and Recreation Commission to ban camping in the area, which had been a legal, cool and relatively unpublicized tradition.

Later that summer, this drama made the evening news in Portland but none of the transplant, big hair anchors had a clue about Oregon's legacy of open beach access and basically reported the story as the fault of miscreants who littered beer cans and syringes and defecated in the dunes without burying their mounds. The phrases "Beach Bill," "Tom McCall," and "public access" were never mentioned. It was some of the worst reporting I've seen, even by vapid local television news standards, and it completely ignored the real issue—who controls the beaches in this state?

As a result of the complaints and after public hearings in Salem and Tillamook, the Oregon Parks and Recreation Department (OPRD) proposed a rule prohibiting camping on the beach and asked for public comments on the idea before the commission decided to adopt the proposal. A few residents who claimed the garbage problem was overblown objected to the ban and one rebel even gathered signatures on a petition requesting an extension of the public comment period.

They received zero support from their coastal lawmakers.

Later that fall, OPRD banned camping on Neahkahnie Beach until a master plan for the Oregon coastline was developed. When that will happen is undetermined and considering the Oregon Legislature's recent budgetary support of

OPRD, the ban may be permanent.

Finally, in spring 2001, the Tillamook County Commission passed an ordinance authorizing the sheriff's department to uphold the ban. A deputy was assigned to patrol the beach, ticket non-conformists, and clean up the problem. That's how it stands in 2003.

I understand the revulsion felt by those who discover waste left behind by overnight beach visitors. It happens to me all the time on Nestucca Spit where I hang out and where it's illegal to camp (and shouldn't be). But I believe the camping ban at Neahkahnie Beach was draconian and a violation of a sacred Oregon ideal. There are so few places left on Oregon's coast to camp legally on the beach. That's not what West and McCall had in mind.

Think about that—very few places to camp on the beach—in Oregon! Let alone free. I'm not talking about paying money and pitching a tent on a paved site ten feet away from 40-foot RVs in the almost corporate atmosphere of mega state parks like Nehalem Bay and Cape Lookout. I'm referring to the special late-night moments on the beach, away from the prudish masses, vehicles, city noises, and temporarily, civilization's refinements.

Think of those impromptu road trips from the Willamette Valley or the debauched local teenage gatherings at secret beach sites. How about all those messed-up people from all over the state? They get into a piece-of-shit car, usually after midnight, sometimes drunk, high, maybe recently fired or dumped, maybe beat-up or having beat someone up,

7

and drive fast and west over the wet Coast Range to the ocean. They roll out a sleeping bag on the public sand and sleep near the Pacific. They wake to the calm gray light on the Oregon Coast hoping to have set things straight. My cousin used to do this kind of thing all the time! I sense it preserved his sanity. These people can't afford motels. They don't want to stay in motels. Many times I have seen these people asleep very early in morning in the dunes at Nestucca Spit, some with only their coat for a cover. Sometimes it's pouring. You want these Oregonians to pay fines?

So many Oregonians have indelible memories from a legal (or illegal) camping experience at the beach. Mine took place after a lie to my mother, some cheap champagne purchased by my older sister, and a night with my girlfriend on the sand near Arcadia Beach State Park just south of Cannon Beach.

These are rites of Oregon passage. Now a few wealthy weekenders in conspiracy with local elected officials have terminated overnight access at Neahkahnie Beach for certain Oregonians to experience these individually created rites. I detect an odor of class bias here and it smells a lot worse that anything a beach camper might leave behind.

Who knows how many folk songs have been sung, first kisses tried, hands-down-the-pants rebuffed, hotdogs roasted, poems composed, bonfires set, bongs loaded, acid dropped, marshmallows burned, jug wine swilled, beers shotgunned, or how many fine Americans were conceived at overnight outings on Neahkahnie Beach.

8

Does that have to go away in this state?

Right now, go out to an Oregon beach and stand there. You'll feel a rumble under the sand that upsets your balance and grows stronger every day, the faster spinning, nearly wrecked, peaceful afterlives of Oswald West and Tom McCall.

The entrance to Bob Straub State Park on Nestucca Spit in Pacific City.

Thank You Bob Straub

A fine Oregonian died last year, former Governor Bob Straub. He wasn't a native, but his excellent public service to this state should qualify him as one. He was the walking, talking, pissing undistilled vinegar, real Beaver State thing. He was imbued or more likely intoxicated by the spirit of William U'Ren, the Oregon politician who created the initiative, referendum and recall processes, collectively known worldwide as the "Oregon System." U'Ren said:

I would go to hell for the people of Oregon.

Bob Straub went to hell for the people of Oregon all

11

right. He once went to Tillamook County to change minds on a land-use planning issue.

The print media ran the proper front-page obituaries. The tributes poured in. Straub's career received its proper due and the brief scrutiny provided a look back at an era of progressive and bipartisan Oregon that today seems as distant as when hominids began to walk upright.

But what about the corporeal decision-making stuff? What about a real example of something tangible this bold, supposedly unpolished, public servant made happen that benefits everyone from, transplanted to, or just visiting Oregon.

I was just there 30 minutes ago.

I was on Nestucca Spit, in Bob Straub State Park near Pacific City, running the length of it with my three dogs like I do two or three times a week.

Dawn was breaking when we hit the packed wet sand. Rain felt imminent. There was no wind. There were no other humans. The dogs of course went nuts. I broke a rule by letting them romp off-leash. Who cared? By the time we made it to magic roiling spot where the Pacific Ocean meets Nestucca Bay, it was full daylight and a couple of harbor seals bobbed 30 feet out. I turned around, took in Cape Kiwanda and Haystack Rock, observed a little illegal campfire smoke in the nearby dunes, and ripped it back up Nestucca Spit with the dogs rumbling in the surf like Steve Prefontaine in high school.

Without Straub there would be a freeway there today. Want to know what it might have looked like? Go to Beverly

Beach north of Newport and check out Highway 101's route there—an unmitigated disaster.

Straub killed the insane Nestucca Highway idea 36 years ago. He slew it for all time, and the story is worth retelling for many compelling reasons, chief among them as a lesson to this generation of Oregon's elected officials. The lesson is—get back to making Oregon distinct.

In 1967, at the zenith of its fanatic Oregon Coast Highway straightening mission, the dictatorial State Highway Commission, (now Oregon Department of Transportation) issued an edict: the state shall reroute Highway 101 north of Beaver and the people shall like it.

The official madness was to plow up farms near Sandlake, pave over parts of the Sandlake Estuary, decapitate the hamlet of Tierra del Mar, pour concrete over McPhillips Beach, blast through Cape Kiwanda, drill pilings into Nestucca Spit, span Nestucca Bay with steel, and dynamite through a headland called Porter Point where hippies picked mushrooms and practiced paganism! Nineteen sixty-seven also happened to be the same year the "Beach Bill" (House Bill 1601) passed the Oregon Legislature by a landslide and Governor Tom McCall signed it into law with great fanfare and a quote from Oswald West about the beaches being a "great birthright" of the Oregon people.

Incredibly, McCall favored the plan. So did many locals. Not Bob Straub. He was appalled, especially because he'd been a key behind-the-scenes player in the successful fight for the "Beach Bill."

13

Only a year earlier, McCall had defeated Straub in the Governor's race and it might have seemed Straub wanted a little payback. It's a lot less conniving than that: Bob Straub simply loved open, public Oregon beaches, loved Pacific City and Nestucca Spit, and loved bringing his family there. So he led the fight to stop it by taking on McCall, and arguably the most powerful unelected politician in the state, Mr. Imperious, Mr. Fixer, Glenn Jackson. Jackson headed the Highway Commission (fiefdom) and had earned a reputation for wanting to limit private development near beaches—so he could build highways down them.

Straub took his case to Washington D.C., to the Secretary of the Interior since the Bureau of Land Management managed a small piece of Nestucca Spit. Straub argued with Governor McCall in public. Straub wrote letters to the editor and held press conferences. And he went to the lion's den in Pacific City in South Tillamook County. It's a place with a pristine stretch of beach framing the Nestucca Estuary that the rerouted super-slabbed highway would have murdered for all time—or at least until the inevitable storm waves carried the concrete away. (The Pacific Ocean breached Nestucca Spit in 1978 in the only known natural breaching of spit on the Pacific Northwest Coast.)

Yes, Straub went to the wet country of dairy and logging and dory boats. There were meetings, and the rancor must have flown like the Columbia River used to. But when the sand settled, and effigies for and against the project were burned in Pacific City, Straub triumphed and won perhaps the greatest environmental victory ever on the Oregon Coast. Nestucca Spit is now and will always be an open beach thanks to him.

Straub was state treasurer at the time. Yes, the state treasurer. I'm an Oregon political junkie and I don't even know the current state treasurer or really what this person does. Perhaps something about the state's bond rating. Perhaps making dubious economic forecasts. Probably behind a desk staring at a flat panel screen. What I do know is that he or she surely wouldn't be out in the country trying to rally citizens to stop an obscenity proposed by another state agency. Is obscenity too strong a word? I've seen the drawings of this highway project. Obscenity may be sugarcoating it.

In the end, the highway wasn't rerouted. It still curves slowly and torturously through Beaver, Hebo, and Cloverdale and completely bypasses Pacific City. So what? If you want to see the beach around there, drive west off Highway 101, park, and get out of your car. Try Bob Straub State Park, renamed for him in 1987. Hike the spit. Walk it. Sprint it. Play football. Throw a Frisbee. Make out. Make love. Get laid. Scream Whitman to the heavens. Run naked lighted by a full moon. Let your dogs run free. Try to tan. Picnic. Drink beer. Smoke a bowl in the dunes. Think. Fish for perch. Ride a horse. Ride a one-speed bike down it and haul out returnable cans and bottles like one dude occasionally does. Gather driftwood. Make an illegal fire. Do nothing useful. Just thank Bob Straub.

Samuel Boardman's car on the Southern Oregon Coast.

Fucking Up

In an anthem off his classic record *Ragged Glory*, Neil Young poses the question: "Why do I keep fucking up?" It's a good personal question. I ask it a lot. Sometimes though, I believe, it's a good thing to change the pronoun and ask the question to a state's citizenry.

The citizens of Oregon have practiced fucking up over the years. They voted down an initiative to ban clearcutting. They repeatedly refuse to legalize marijuana. They return Republican incumbents to the Oregon Legislature. They don't seize once-in-a-lifetime opportunities to place large tracts of the undeveloped Oregon Coast permanently in the public trust.

On the subject of the latter, in 1936, 1940, and 1968, Oregonians fucked up. Collectively these incidents amount to one astonishing and colossal coastal fuck up that still haunts the state.

Today hardly anyone remembers these three events. I study Oregon history for a literary living and they were unknown to me until not long ago when I unearthed and read three obscure books that revealed the story. I resurrect it now because sometimes Americans can learn lessons from blatantly stupid, shortsighted or immoral acts practiced by a preceding generation, like damming the Snake River, segregating schools, napalming villages, and sterilizing the mentally retarded. A citizenry can only be judged by the quality of its last worst decision. The point is to get better. Sadly, in this Oregon case, it's too late to get better. Self-flagellation, however, sometimes does serve a useful purpose.

Chapter six of Thomas R. Cox's *The Park Builders: A History of State Parks in the Pacific Northwest* details part one of the fuck up.

In 1936, Samuel Boardman, Oregon's first State Parks Superintendent, proposed a bold and visionary plan: to expand the park system, the state would float bonds to finance the purchase of undeveloped private land along the Oregon Coast.

Boardman wasn't after just any property. He specifically wanted to buy up all the narrow strips of land between the Roosevelt Highway (now Highway 101) and the beach, which the state already owned. These strips varied in size from 50 to 1000 feet, depending on how close the highway was to the shore. If you examine an Oregon Coast highway map from that era, we're talking about a lot of natural space.

This was the golden age of acquisition for public recreation space in Oregon. Boardman recognized that the time was now or never for the state to buy up undeveloped land near the beach. The problem that faced Boardman was obvious. His new agency barely had a budget, and the rural-dominated Legislature loathed the idea of spending money to buy land in general and especially during the Depression.

Almost all of this land was undeveloped wetlands, diked floodplains (for grazing) or shifting dunes that had yet to be planted with European beach grass for stabilization. Boardman calculated that all the land, potentially thousands of acres, could be bought for $500,000. Half a million dollars. Most of these parcels were owned by cash-poor coastal landowners getting beat up by the Depression or Portlanders no longer financially secure after the 1929 stock market crash. Both types would have willingly sold their holdings for cheap had the state made offers.

Boardman's bond idea went nowhere.

Once World War II started, the economy boomed and land prices climbed, livestock commodities gained value, and farmers, speculators, sportsmen, developers, timber companies, and engineers came in to exploit, run more cows, drain more marshes, level forests, fish harder, and build, build, build, liquidate, liquidate, liquidate. The window to cheaply buy undeveloped land near the Oregon Coast had closed forever.

Think of that. For 500 grand (just over $6 million today adjusted for inflation) Oregon could have frozen part of its coast in time and preserved it as one of the most progressive and ecologically sensitive places in North America. There was still plenty of land left in the area to profitably continue the natural resource extraction and tourism industries. This acquisition could have gone a long way in preventing so many of the intractable environmental problems that confound the region today: flooding, loss of key estuarine habitat for salmonids, terrible water quality, riprapping shifting sand dunes, and acres and acres of tawdry, ill-conceived development.

It also would have looked pretty damn good to see wetlands where cows now shit and deserted sand spits where 4000-square foot "homes" occupied a few weeks out of the year now taint the landscape.

Boardman failed in 1936. But he wouldn't give up. That same losing year he pitched another bold coastal preservation idea. Four years later it went down too. This defeat is part two of the fucking up and it's all recounted dryly and ugly in *Oregon's Highway Park System: 1929-1989, An Administrative History*, (many contributing writers).

Today it blows one's Oregonian mind to imagine what Boardman conceived and very nearly pulled off. He wanted to turn most of the remote Curry County shoreline on the Southern Oregon Coast into a national park that would rival both the famed Redwoods National Park to the south and the roadless coastal strip of Washington's awesomely unspoiled Olympic National Park to the north.

To push his idea, Boardman hustled, wrote reams of

letters, prayed, cajoled politicians, met with the Secretary of the Interior, and toured federal bureaucrats around the area, which was practically deserted and inaccessible at the time. Boardman's multiple assault strategy apparently worked because the Secretary of the Interior and National Park Service approved his plan for a National Recreation Area, then a precursor to national park status. US Senator Charles McNary from Oregon introduced a bill containing a funding provision for land acquisition but some lackey in the Bureau of the Budget eliminated the provision. The idea stalled at that point and the ensuing vacuum allowed a few local livestock ranchers to emerge and oppose it over the potential loss of grazing land. The stockmen prevailed and killed in perpetuity Boardman's brilliant plan to preserve a beautiful and pristine 40-mile, say again—40-mile!—stretch of Oregon coastal landscape. All because of cows.

Years later Oregon acquired some of the land in the area envisioned for Oregon's second national park and named a state park after Boardman, a cosmic backhanded compliment to a great dead man if there ever was such a thing.

Today a rerouted Highway 101 plows right through Samuel Boardman State Park and there's grotesque development, including a gated resort at the southern end, a cosmic middle finger to a great dead man if there ever was such a thing.

Well above Samuel Boardman State Park, at 1700 feet on the old crooked Coast Highway in Carpenterville, looking north, west, and south, a person can imagine what a national park would have looked like: virtually no roads, no logging, no trophy homes, no cows, no fences, no rerouted and slabbed Highway 101.

A tattered edition of the *Oregon Voters Pamphlet* revealed fuck up part three.

In 1968 a constitutional amendment by initiative appeared on the Oregon ballot. If passed by the voters it would have authorized the state to establish a temporary fund to acquire beach access points and recreational easement rights on privately owned beaches. To do so, the amendment would have raised the gas tax one cent per gallon on passenger vehicles for three years, 1969-72. The initiative also prohibited highway construction on beaches.

It was all necessary because the "Beach Bill," (House Bill 1601) which Governor McCall had signed into law only a year earlier, faced a state *and* federal court challenge largely on Fifth Amendment claims against the government seizure of private property without just compensation. The passage of the "Beach Bill" had been a big deal and made most Oregonians feel good, but the reality was that the state appeared powerless to stop development in the disputed dry sand areas until the courts weighed in. In the interim however, and nobody knew how long that might last, people could exploit the Oregon Coast landscape with impunity, and that's exactly what a few developer types did.

The situation called for some kind of daring preemptive action and a leader who stood for much more than the pedestrian and soulless nature of putting private property

22

"rights" first in every public policy decision.

Enter State Treasurer Bob Straub. His group called Beaches Forever Inc. (!) and the initiative idea. Activists gathered 90,000 signatures (unpaid) to qualify a piece of progressive direct democracy for the ballot. The proposed law was absolutely brilliant how it played to private landowners' self-interest while hoping in the end to service a larger public and environmental good.

The amendment was simple, easy for the public to understand, asked something of them but not much, attempted to preserve something special for their children's future, clearly showed where the money was coming from and where it would go, and perhaps most importantly, contained a sunset provision. It would also, if passed, render any court decision overturning the "Beach Bill," basically moot since the state would simply pay up.

In the pamphlet, Beaches Forever Inc. (probably Straub), argued:

> *We must act NOW. The Oregon beaches are in jeopardy. Real estate promoters want to exploit them...as an exclusive playground for the few who can afford their extravagant resorts. Private cabanas, no-trespassing signs, fences and concrete will destroy the dry sand area where Oregonians have been free to play for generations.*

Six weeks before the election, a poll revealed voters

supported the initiative by a staggering 85 percent. Then something slithered out from under a rock in the form of an organization called The Family Highway Protection Council (FHPC). It blitzed the state with radio and television spots, and direct mail objecting to the one-cent tax. Later in the campaign it was learned that a consortium of American oil companies had put up $89,930 to fund FHPC. It was the only money raised or spent to defeat the initiative. Not one cent came from Oregon.

FHPC's efforts quickly eroded public support. Rarely had Oregonians seen such a slick and withering attack. Two weeks before the election Governor McCall finally swung his full support behind the initiative. Had he come out in favor earlier, his influence might have carried the day. But the man who signed the "Beach Bill" into law with great fanfare was too late.

It went down 464,140 to 315,175 in a blowout. One commentator would later write the public turnaround on the initiative ranks, "…among the most remarkable phenomenons in Oregon history." It was brought to us by oil companies and Oregon voters. That tops even cows.

Neil, I know the answer to your question if I ask it about myself. I don't know about Oregon's citizenry when it comes to their shoreline.

A 1978 pamphlet published by the State of Oregon.

A Coastal Sweep

Game 1

I've got a good lie in the Sandtrap Lounge at the Gearhart Golf Links. Outside I see large white men afflicted with hooks and shanks and oozing bad scores. Across from me sits an Oregon hero. We drink excellent Bombay Sapphire martinis. I bought the best because he deserves the best. He practically saved the Oregon Coast from Southern Californication 36 years ago. I looked him up to say "thanks" and we're here drinking his favorite cocktail. It's on me. All his drinks should be on Oregonians who love the beach. It behooves the state to rename a coastal park for him, and a big one too, not a puny paved wayside. I'm about ready to order another round of Bombays, maybe doubles. I'm that thankful. When they arrive, I'll feel like standing on the table, clinking my glass with a spoon, point to a hero, and telling the golfers a story.

His name is Dr. Bob Bacon. He lives in Gearhart. I first became acquainted with him on a summer afternoon in 2002 at a ceremony marking the 35th anniversary of the "Beach Bill," the landmark 1967 law that politicians like to take credit for and certain environmentalists still gorge themselves on. At the ceremony, held inexplicably at the Salishan Resort, Dr. Bacon told a brief, modest story about his role in passage of the "Beach Bill" that blew away Governor Kitzhaber's lengthy, oral valentine to himself about handling the New Carissa shipwreck.

As it turns out, the story wasn't so modest. At stake in the drama was nothing less than the very soul of the Oregon Coast. Dr. Bacon just told the story with modesty. As I listened to him that afternoon, it occurred to me that almost everything I knew about the struggle to pass the "Beach Bill" was not so much wrong, just overemphasized. And that overemphasis centered exclusively on Tom McCall.

It was the summer of 66' on a clam tide that it all began. Tom McCall wasn't even governor yet.

A Portland couple picnicked on Cannon Beach in front of the Surfsand Motel, owned by William Hay. A motel employee told them to leave, citing a nearby sign that read: "Surfsand guests only." They left, shaken, and reported the incident to their nephew, Lawrence Bitte, a graduate student in biochemistry at Oregon Medical School (now OHSU) where Dr. Bacon had been a Professor of Anatomy since 1955. Bitte wrote letters of complaint to then-Secretary of State Tom McCall, who passed them over to the Oregon Highway Department, the agency then in charge of state parks. Investigators paid a visit to the Surfsand and reported back to their superiors. A shock of awareness bolted through the agency: *what was happening at the Surfsand could happen everywhere on the Oregon Coast.*

Hay's crude policy towards "trespassers" outraged officials but Highway Department lawyers concluded it was probably legal since control of the dry sands area above the median high tide line had never been firmly established by law. By custom this section of beach belonged to the people, who had recreated there freely since the state was settled. Nothing in statute explicitly guaranteed this however, or prevented development of what was essentially private property. Suddenly, the long-ingrained popular notion of open Oregon beaches was imperiled. Highway Department lawyers quickly drafted a bill that would establish state control of the disputed dry sands area and readied it for the 1967 legislative session. Eventually this piece of legislation became known as House Bill 1601—the "Beach Bill."

The bill landed in the House Highway Committee, a group dominated by rural Republicans, including a couple of coastal Neanderthals. There, the bill promptly stalled. Bitte grew impatient and nervous over its status. He shared his concern with Dr. Bob Bacon and they decided to "get down to Salem and see what was happening." At the last minute Bitte couldn't go because of a critical research assignment, so Dr. Bacon and Bitte's wife, Diane, drove to the Capitol.

"We didn't even know how to really get there," he said. They didn't know where the House Highway Committee convened. They didn't know if there was even a hearing on the bill scheduled.

After being told by a Capitol staffer that no such bill about beaches existed, Dr. Bacon learned that the Highway Committee was in session—at that very moment. In fact, the bill they had come to check out was on the docket and being discussed—right then. He also learned this was to be the last session on this particular bill. "It was a total fluke," Dr. Bacon said.

It was nearing lunch when Dr. Bacon and Diane poked their head in and sat down in the back of the hearing room. The committee was ready to wrap up the matter and table the bill since the motel owners and developers had already testified how very bad the bill was for their future. There had been no speakers in favor of the bill aside from Highway Department employees. Committee Chairman Sidney Bazett noticed the strangers and invited them to return after lunch. When the committee reconvened, Bazett announced, without consultation, that the presence of two citizens indicated a public interest in the legislation and the public should be heard from. He invited Dr. Bacon to come back to Salem and testify.

"There was a general 'Oh shit!' look from the rest of

28

the committee when Bazett said this," recalled Dr. Bacon.

Dr. Bacon had four days to get something together, four days to galvanize an Oregon public oblivious to what was at stake. He was teaching a full load. He had zero experience in political organizing. He wasn't even political by nature. There was no money, office or extra phone lines. He wasn't sure if he knew the names of his state representative or senator. There were no environmental pros to tell him what to do. Dr. Bacon simply went to work on instinct.

When it was all over, he and his crew made Oregon history.

A press conference was called and State Treasurer Bob Straub shared the podium with Bitte. They declared the inalienable Oregon right to enjoy open beaches was in grave jeopardy. Matt Kramer, an Associated Press reporter, caught wind of the story and started cranking out the copy. He moved the issue to the front page of Willamette Valley newspapers. He was the first to call HB 1601 the "Beach Bill" and it stuck. Dr. Bacon hooked up with a political animal named Ken Fitzgerald who just happened to live at the Oregon Coast. They visited the news manager of KGW television and briefed him on the issue. He decided to deliver an editorial alerting Oregonians about the imminent threat to their beaches. He opened it silently with a long shot of a drawing of a fence around Haystack Rock. He said this would happen if Oregonians didn't speak up. He told them to contact their lawmakers—now!

Oregonians went nuts on an issue like never before.

29

Within days of the broadcast they sent a record 35,000 pieces of mail to Salem. These weren't canned emails. These were pissed-off Oregonians demanding action. Coastal bumpkins cried it was slickers from the Willamette Valley raising a fuss. Fitzgerald countered by organizing hundreds of coastal locals to caravan to the Capitol steps. Subsequent hearings on HB 1601 were packed and video monitors had to be set up in the halls to accommodate the overflow. A name emerged: Citizens to Save Oregon Beaches—the SOBs. People began to volunteer. Bacon hit the rubber chicken circuit and did radio call-in shows all over the state. He gave interview after interview. He made hundreds of phone calls. He never missed a class. His superiors intimated that perhaps he should concentrate more on his profession. Dr. Bacon ignored them. He was inspired by his time spent as a young man in the untainted Adirondacks and he wanted Oregon beaches preserved. He was working around the clock. His doctor told him to take it easy. He refused.

A momentum for the bill had started like a tank dropped from 10,000 feet. It was pure political gravity of the type that squashes self-interest and little minds. House Highway Committee members began to feel the weight ready to flatten and they ran. Dr. Bacon briefed Tom McCall. The new governor hadn't done a damn thing up to this point. He heard a royal bandwagon about ready to pass him by. He staged his dramatic helicopter landings on the Oregon Coast and got into the game, pretty much in the fourth quarter.

Dr. Bacon was amused at the Governor's ploy, but "it

had its impact." McCall was welcomed as an ally and his stunt dynamited the bill out of the committee. It passed the House 57-3. Then the Senate took a run at it to clear up some murky legal questions. In a matter of weeks, the "Beach Bill" had gone from receiving the last rites to a holy legislative resurrection. It had become *the* issue of the 1967 session and everyone wanted a piece of the credit.

Still there were dark and pustular forces that wanted the sands for themselves and cabanas. Dr. Bacon recalled hearing about state lawmakers having egregious conflicts of interest regarding undeveloped coastal property in the disputed dry sands area. In a dive Portland bar he met a state senator who wanted him to sign off on a watered-down beach protection bill. Dr. Bacon refused. The senator exploded, "We'll see who owns the Oregon beaches!" One night Dr. Bacon received a call from the wife of a coastal motel owner. She had overheard from local developer/motel interests that suitcases of cash from Reno and San Francisco were heading north for some "unofficial lobbying." She didn't agree with the "Beach Bill" but bribery was crossing the line.

After some tweaking by the Senate, the "Beach Bill" passed that chamber in a landslide. It went back to the House and they overwhelmingly approved an amended version that empowered the state to control the disputed dry sands area. A few coastal lawmakers still balked, but by that time, after being pancaked by the fallen tank, they'd learned that Oregon's beaches aren't a fiefdom where serfs can be denied access to surf. The beaches belong to all Oregonians.

31

Governor McCall signed the "Beach Bill" with flourish and made a great speech.

"There was a sense of relief," Dr. Bacon said. "Everyone sort of collapsed and I suspect the martinis were flowing."

Yes, I'm in the Sandtrap Lounge with an Oregon hero, Dr. Bob Bacon. We didn't down a second round of Bombays. The first one pretty much kicked our ass. I also didn't stand on the table and call attention to Dr. Bacon's role in the "Beach Bill" story. That's not really keeping with his self-effacing style. His reward is a pitching wedge away from his front door—open Oregon beaches forever. He also has the satisfaction of receiving something special from another Oregonian. In November of 1982, Tom McCall, wracked with terminal cancer, sent Dr. Bacon a Christmas card. It read: "Better early than never." He wasn't referring to Christmas.

Game 2

Nixon had just crushed McGovern. A young married couple stood in the living room of a house on seven acres on the North Oregon Coast. They were signing the deed when the realtor looked out a window, across Highway 101, to a sliver of the property, and said, "You know, that little piece of land you own is going to be worth a lot more if PGE builds that nuclear power plant there."

Not more than a half mile in front of the house and obliterating the view of the ocean, a nuclear reactor on a

32

tightly secured industrial site.

Katharine and Goodwin Harding fell silent, stunned. It was the first time either one of them had heard about the project. They signed anyway. This was before Three Mile Island, *The China Syndrome*, *Silkwood*, the *No Nukes* concert film and classic double album, the Washington Public Power Supply System (Whoops) debt fiasco, and of course, Chernobyl and human mutants.

A year later the plan for a nuclear power plant on a scenic section of the Cascadia subduction zone were dead. The Hardings murdered it.

It was November 22, 1972. The Hardings, both 25, were set to buy a 1937 farmhouse just north of Neskowin that once belonged to a master cheese grader named Christensen, whose hard-assed commitment to quality made the Tillamook brand famous. In 1970, with unassailable hippie credentials, the Hardings had driven a VW bus to the Northwest from the Northeast. They visited the Oregon Coast via the Wilson River Highway, fell in love with the land and seascapes, and decided to stay.

First they lived in an old CCC cabin up the Nestucca River for $40 a month and were befriended by Mennonite neighbors. Later they rented a house just north of Neskowin until it burned down. After the fire and the unexpected outpouring of community support, they lived for a short time in a teepee while they searched for a place to buy.

Soon they found one, the home where this nuclear

33

tale begins. "I knew the first minute I walked in it was the place we wanted," Katherine said standing in the same house she and Goodwin have lived in for over 30 years and raised three children.

The plant's demise started the moment the realtor left, no doubt ecstatic over his commission on a $26,000 sale. Within days, 20 people, none of whom were born and raised in the area, gathered at the Harding's home, formed the Community of Atomic Study (COAST) and decided to fight a proposed nuclear power plant in Tillamook County.

Goodwin was appointed president, Katharine librarian, and a few bucks were raised. Although the Hardings had participated in several anti-Vietnam War marches on the East Coast, they had zero experience in organizing protests. At their first meeting, Katharine recalled it was obvious the group knew very little about Portland General Electric's (PGE) plans and absolutely nothing about nuclear power. They didn't know that PGE had decided in 1970 to site a nuclear power plant near the Oregon Coast and kept it relatively secret from the general coastal public. They also didn't know that apparently every elected official who represented Tillamook County at the local, state and federal level knew about the plan and favored it.

After investigating four possible sites around the county, PGE dropped the Harding area from consideration (and others near Rockaway and the Nehalem Bay Estuary) and acquired options to purchase 720 acres northwest of Miles Lake, about two miles north of Cape Kiwanda. PGE then blitzed the area with propaganda, including a pro-nuke pep assembly for Nestucca High School students.

PGE claimed the project offered clean, safe energy, no ugly cooling towers (they'd be using ocean water instead), 1000 temporary jobs, 75 permanent ones, an annual payroll of $1.5 million, and an eventual staggering property tax valuation for the plant of $600 million, which was three times the total value of assessed property in Tillamook County! Concerning potential damage to the local environment, PGE speculated that thermal discharge to the ocean would actually enhance marine life and improve fisheries, which was especially good news to Pacific City's famed dory boat fishing fleet.

Most South Tillamook County residents swallowed the bait and drummed up support through letters to the Tillamook newspaper and by packing public meetings. It seemed clear that a majority of people from the area wanted the plant, the jobs, the tax revenue, and were ignorant or apathetic about the potential risks of nuclear power.

So were many Americans.

This was the golden era of nuclear power plant construction in the United States. The Pacific Northwest, despite being blessed with cheap hydroelectric power, happily jumped on board the atomic bandwagon. The Bonneville Power Administration issued a study that envisioned up to 25 nuclear power plants in the region and an incredible 50,000 high-paying jobs. In 1968 near the town of Rainier on the Columbia River, PGE broke ground on its state-of-the-art Trojan facility, a 1,130 megawatt power plant that was the darling of the industry and had the distinction of being praised by then-Undersecretary of the Interior James Watt as "particularly attractive environmentally." PGE even retained the services of famed architect Pietro Belluschi to advise how the plant's design, especially the massive cooling towers, could best be integrated aesthetically into the landscape.

COAST knew its first order of business, a quick and rigorous self-education about every aspect of nuclear power. They poured over documents, studies, articles, books, and talked to experts, including one from the Livermore Laboratory. It was a crash-hard science course for a bunch of liberal arts majors, and after "graduation" they produced a 30-page pamphlet titled *Nuclear Power in Tillamook County*. It sold for 50 cents and was so thorough and readable that it generated requests for distribution from all around the country, including a church in rural Nevada. "We have no idea how the word about the pamphlet got out," Katharine said.

COAST hardly limited itself to a pamphlet (which they mailed to practically every important legislator in the state). They drew up a long list of protest actions and within a few months checked them all off. COAST wrote letters to newspapers and elected officials. (Governor Tom McCall wrote back, "...nuclear power is the best alternative, so far as I can see.") They contacted friends and family in high places, including a father on PGE's board. They set up a booth at the county fair that a visiting Senator Mark Hatfield conspicuously avoided. They held public forums and barnstormed the county's rubber chicken circuit with a 16-mm anti-nuke film and borrowed projector to give presentations about the perils of atomic power. At one Elks or Rotary or VFW meeting, Goodwin doesn't remember the group, he and a colleague were greeted by a room full of old timers soaked on Jack Daniel's. Goodwin rolled the film and made his pitch.

In addition to taking the show on the road, COAST formed alliances with other activist groups. They gathered signatures for a petition demanding a moratorium on new nuclear power plant construction. They posted hundreds of flyers headlined, "You vs. the Atom—It's Possible to Win." They testified at legislative hearings and Goodwin cut his hair to come across less radical. COAST was so determined that they even held a meeting on Super Bowl Sunday—during the game!

At first COAST felt apart from many of the locals, but Katharine remembered some of the long-term residents eventually joining the effort once the truth about nuclear power on the Oregon Coast emerged. COAST's positive political strategies starkly contrasted with much of the in-your-face protest of the early 1970s. These volatile strategies perhaps worked elsewhere but this was the North Oregon Coast, specifically Tillamook County. COAST asked tough questions, pushed education, maintained a professional public demeanor, and employed savvy media relations. They knew the key to victory was successfully lobbying the people with the power to ultimately approve the plant. That wasn't the local residents. Why antagonize them? Why not reach out to them?

COAST was organized, indefatigable and civil, even

when answering charges they were, "too young, outsiders, dilettantes, a lunatic fringe, ecology freaks, and un-American." In the midst of this grueling grassroots political protest, they learned something about channeling the free-floating anger of the era into local positive activism. "Before all of this," Goodwin said, "I would have never gone to a zoning meeting. But it's about going up to Tillamook 30 miles away with 12 people on a rainy night and speaking up...because if you don't, maybe no one else will."

The plan to site a nuclear power plant on the Oregon Coast ended quietly in the fall of 1973. Katharine recalled there was no formal announcement from PGE or celebration by the victors. "One day we just heard it was over," she said.

COAST had won. A power company had lost in an era when power companies never lost. Later the Hardings discovered through their PGE board contact that *local opposition* had made the difference in the decision to pull out. "You" had beaten the "Atom."

Game 3

In 1978, something called the Governor's Task Force on Outer Continental Shelf Oil and Gas Development published an 8 1/2" by 9" 54-page pamphlet titled *Oregon and offshore oil*. Twenty-five years later I excavated a three-dollar copy from an Oregon Coast thrift store.

Who knows what *Oregon and offshore oil's* press run was or how it was distributed. Its initial release came 117 years after the first commercial oil well, five years after the

Arab oil embargo and humbling gas lines, and 25 years before the American invasion of Iraq, which instantly dropped the price of a barrel of oil.

The top half of the pamphlet's cover is Texas-tea black. The bottom half is Douglas fir-Oregon green. A lowercase, cream-colored "oregon" in a fat, round 1970s-style font separates the black from the green. The black at the top appears ready to spill over the green at the bottom. The word "oregon" dams the black away from the green. There's a black line drawing of an offshore oil platform inside the second "o" of "oregon." Below the "g" and surrounded by green is the black-colored phrase, "and offshore oil."

Connie Morehouse designed the cover. At first glance it struck me as a masterpiece on every subconscious and subversive graphic design level. How it passed muster from her pro-oil superiors is a miracle. Maybe she was one of those folks who actually listened to President Jimmy Carter when he asked Americans to turn down their thermostats and wear sweaters. He also created the Department of Energy and pushed for the research and development of alternative fuels. He's considered a joke by the current American junta.

The interregnum from the 1973 embargo when President Nixon governed, to the 2003 invasion when a Nixon lackey's son reigned, marks an era distinguished by the greatest failure of public policy, national security and executive leadership in the second half of this country's existence. (It was slavery/botched Reconstruction the first half.)

Of course that American failure is the prolonged, gov-

39

ernment-subsidized and insane addiction to fossil fuels.

Oregon and offshore oil opens with the riff, "...Oregon's role in the unfolding energy drama may soon change." Over the next 51 pages the pamphlet describes how this drama might play out off Oregon's shoreline since federal law ceded control of submerged lands up to three miles from shore to individual states.

Oregon and offshore oil piles on the propaganda in a first-person Oregonian voice. It addresses potential environmental problems and reassures they won't happen because Oregon especially values its natural environment. A case is made that offshore rigs actually benefit marine life by creating artificial reefs. The pamphlet presents an economic multiplier model with a promise of many permanent living-wage jobs on the hard-up Oregon Coast. It displays a reassuring photograph of Governor Bob Straub in a pinstripe suit and hardhat with his former environmental nemesis, state highway dictator Glenn Jackson, visiting what appears to be an offshore oil platform. There's another photograph of a blowout preventer. *Oregon and offshore oil* concludes with a glossary of oil production terms, a reading reference list, and "A Call to Oregon Citizens," seeking input and imploring Oregonians to consider, "...what each one of us can do now to conserve energy."

Big Oil conducted exploratory drilling off Oregon at seven sites in 1964-65. Initial test results disappointed. Big Oil never gives up. Thus, 14 years later the state published *Oregon and offshore oil* with encouraging sentences like, "The thick sediments located off the Columbia River's mouth and near Newport and Coos Bay may be likely sites." Presumably Oregon officials distributed the pamphlet to soften potential resistance, which figured to be stiff since it was the tail end of Oregon's great run as the national model for implementing aggressive conservation measures. One could also speculate *Oregon and offshore oil* served as a valentine to Big Oil and the federal government, a valentine hinting Oregon wanted drilling.

In 1977, a year before *Oregon and offshore oil*'s publication, the Bureau of Land Management (BLM) ranked the Oregon and Washington continental shelf as lowest "among all the areas in terms of its resource potential and desirability for leasing." Consequently, the region was dropped from a schedule prioritizing offshore drilling sites.

Governor Straub asked the BLM to reconsider. When the pamphlet came out, BLM had apparently not reversed the ranking and the prospect of several platforms in the Columbia River Estuary (one of the glossary terms) seemed remote. Yet a person wouldn't gather that from reading *Oregon and offshore oil*. It makes oil production feel like a done deal, an arranged marriage, complete with a blessing and dowry from Governor Straub, a leader who had previously demonstrated an uncompromising stance when it came to protecting the environment.

Oregon and offshore oil's propaganda mission failed. Today there are no platforms off Oregon's shoreline or in the estuaries. Big Oil didn't get to drill the Beaver State. In 1982

Congress enacted a ban on any new offshore oil drilling. By then it was too late for places like the Gulf of Mexico, but Oregon's coastal communities were saved from Louisianafication. What possessed Oregon public officials to consider oil production off Oregon's famed open and relatively untainted beaches. A possession? More likely it was a State of Oregon fugue.

A fugue is defined as: "a disturbed state of consciousness in which the one affected seems to perform acts in full awareness but upon recovery cannot recollect the deeds."

A fugue can return. Big Oil never gives up.

From the June 13, 2003 *Oregonian*:

Senate seeks inventory of offshore reserves

WASHINGTON – The Senate on Thursday called for a comprehensive inventory of offshore oil and gas resources, turning aside concerns that the effort might lead to energy development in coastal waters closed to drilling for two decades.

Jo, Ray and Sonny romping at low tide on Whalen Island.

What Men Can't Tell You at Lake Success

To me a park is a pulpit

Samuel Boardman, father of the Oregon state park system

Not too long ago I visited Whalen Island, Oregon's newest state park, established in early 2000. I was in need of something.

With my three dogs, I walked around the island at low tide on a gorgeous day and soaked up this unique natural space in South Tillamook County on the Oregon Coast. I saw a harbor seal, ravens, a bald eagle and no other humans. I love not seeing humans when I'm walking an Oregon Coast beach. To me, it feels better than seeing wildlife.

At Whalen Island I got what I needed. Sometimes you

can get what you want and what you need.

Even though I was in an awesome, untainted, public site, my mind couldn't stop drifting towards unseemly artifice—meaning Oregon politics and the recent murder of the state by elected officials. I thank all those solons in Salem who over the last two legislative sessions worked so hard to raise highway speed limits, limit abortion, post the Ten Commandments in public school classrooms, support cockfighting, declare hatchery fish wild, provide financing for a baseball stadium, and let sick people die.

I also thought about the excellent public servant Samuel Boardman, who served from 1929 to 1950 as Oregon's first State Park Superintendent and once took a pay cut to keep his office going during the Depression when the idea of the state government buying private land for parks was inconceivable and practically dangerous. He's rightly considered the "Father" of the Oregon state parks system and surely and single-handedly preserved more natural space in Oregon, close to 50,000 acres, than anyone else. If the US Constitution didn't prohibit the states from issuing their own currencies, Boardman's face and one of the great places he saved from pavement would be on both sides of Oregon's dollar bill. I rank him as one of the greatest Oregonians.

So on Whalen Island, surrounded by water and wildlife, thinking about a special Oregonian and public servant, I exorcised the Oregon Legislature from my mind. I also felt called to bear witness. So here's a sermon, sort of, from a preacher's kid, inspired from the pulpit of Whalen Island, in the spirit of Samuel Boardman:

Not all is bad in the world or our small wet corner of it, when a natural space as fine as Whalen Island is permanently placed in the public trust and protected from the prospect of 4000-square foot vacation homes or an RV park decorated with an array of satellite dishes, pop machines, dumpsters and propane tanks.

Back in 2000, two sisters, Karen DeRungs of Tillamook and Kathleen Shaw of Beaverton, sold their 180-acre stake in Whalen Island in the Sandlake Estuary to the Oregon Parks and Recreation Department (OPRD) for $2.8 million. Five other acres of the island are currently operated as a county park and it's probable that one day OPRD will acquire that property too and roll the entire island into the state park.

That's great news, worth celebrating with excessive Keith Richards-like behavior. Now for the hangover. Whalen Island was the first new park on the Oregon Coast with overnight camping facilities since Cape Blanco opened in 1971.

This is incredible, inexcusable, nearly criminal, considering the once-progressive history and international reputation of Oregon's state park development, specifically the coastal park system. Foreign governments used to send their bureaucrats to the Oregon Coast to learn how to do parks right.

Think of what has been lost since 1971. There were huge undeveloped tracts available, particularly the headlands, for a price. Maybe some deals would have amounted to extortion. So what? It's an investment in the state. Oregon experienced record economic growth in the 1990s and mailed tax "kicker" rebate checks. There was a population boom, a massive surge in outdoor recreation, and obviously a need for more state parks.

Yet in this time, OPRD imposed and raised fees, deferred maintenance and made virtually no new land acquisitions. Not so old timers can remember when state parks were free! I'm pushing 40 and can recall that most parks I visited as a child with my family didn't cost a cent to enjoy, let alone take a piss.

What happened to this state's commitment to parks? Where did the appropriations go? Why did Oregon voters approve a ballot measure in 1980 prohibiting the use of gas tax revenue for parks, thereby signaling the end of a progressive agency? Why do I have to pay the dreaded "day-use user fee" if I want to walk my dogs or take a nap in many coastal parks. Where are the champions for parks in the legislative and executive branches? Why can I still use an Oregon parks map from 1969 I recently came across? Why did Oregon Republican legislators hijack Measure 66, the 1998 initiative voters passed in a landslide that was supposed to earmark lottery money for park land acquisitions and improvements? Why did these politicians get away with it? I don't want ideology, personal agendas and hack partisanship from legislators. I want more parks! And if the government wants to raise my taxes or float bonds to pay for them—then do it! Who's going to turn out an incumbent because she supported parks? So many questions, outrages, and pooling black bile, but I don't want to fulminate. I want to think about what Oregon won by buying Whalen Island.

I don't know the details of the negotiations for the land, but according to press reports, the sisters turned down better offers from developers and suggestions from local political mountebanks that the property would better serve the county if developed and on the tax rolls. Furthermore, this also wasn't one of those dubious land swaps made with timber companies that have come under fire recently for ripping off taxpayers and threatening watersheds. This was good all the way around and don't Oregonians wish we could say that about anything connected to Oregon state government in these dark feckless days? Well, go to Whalen Island and say, "This was good." You'll feel better.

Preserving Whalen Island is a net gain for conservation and outdoor recreation and every citizen should heartily thank the sisters. They continue the fine tradition established during the Depression of Oregonians (typically Portlanders) selling or donating their land to the state so all the public can benefit. Sure the sisters got paid a lot, but their decision to sell—below market price—created a legacy for their family. On my karma scorecard that tallies many, many more points than pushing through a gated residential development or golf course in a sensitive natural area and then naming the desecration after a geographical point on the East Coast or a Scottish spelling of a meteorological term. There's a lesson here for other Oregonians who own natural areas near the Pacific Ocean. It's an old one but it needs to be told again and again and beaten into the propertied class. The lesson is this: no one remembers you for building something on the Oregon Coast. They only remember you if you don't.

Turning Whalen Island into a state park is a positive story, but it gets even better

It seems OPRD plans to wisely confine camping on Whalen Island to the already developed five-acre plot that comprises the county park. In other words, there won't be extensive construction to accommodate more motor vehicles and more overnight camping. The agency tentatively plans to do something different here, which means building a few low impact hiking/biking trails lightly marked by interpretative panels teaching estuarine ecology and hopefully some anecdotes about the unique role the coastal parks system have played in Oregon's civic history.

Finally, there's an even happier ending to this story than could ever be imagined by writers of romantic fiction. I have two friends, Will and Debbie Dillon, who live in the woods near Cloverdale. In 1980 they moved to the Oregon Coast and lived in a tent on Whalen Island for four months. Debbie boarded a horse boarded there and both she and Will worked a bit for the mother of the daughters who sold the land to the state.

Times were changing though. Ronald Reagan would be elected in a landslide that fall, James Watt became his Secretary of the Interior, The War on Drugs unconstitutionally declared, and the 1960s definitely over. Nevertheless, Will and Debbie carried on with the counterculture tradition and continued to live a life close to the land. "We were the last hippies, a dying breed," said Will.

A few months after they left the place that's now a state park, the Dillons had their first child, a daughter. They named her Island. A few years went by and a son was born. His name is Whalen. Later Will and Debbie had another daughter and now all of them can go together and experience a landscape as it was when the family began. "It's a godsend," said Will about the new park. "It is a big part of our lives."

Samuel Boardman wrote about Oregon: "Keep it immaculate for the whisper in the treetops tells you what men can't tell you at Lake Success."

Amen Samuel.

He continued: "The quiet of a wooded lake takes you from the hum of Main Street, and the spiritual side of your being is atoned."

I got it at Whalen Island.

Finally, "Might not the answers of a distressed world be found in the God-given sermonettes of a park system?"

Yes.

49

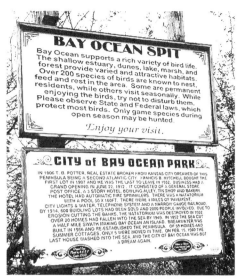

BAY OCEAN SPIT

Bay Ocean supports a rich variety of bird life. The shallow estuary, dunes, lake, marsh, and forest provide varied and attractive habitats. Over 200 species of birds are known to nest, feed and rest in the area. Some are permanent residents, while others visit seasonally. While enjoying the birds, try not to disturb them. Please observe State and Federal laws, which protect most birds. Only game species during open season may be hunted.

Enjoy your visit.

CITY of BAY OCEAN PARK

IN 1906 T. B. POTTER, REAL ESTATE BROKER FROM KANSAS CITY DREAMED OF THIS PENINSULA BEING A SECOND ATLANTIC CITY. FRANCIS B. MITCHELL BOUGHT THE FIRST LOT IN 1907 AND HE WAS THE LAST TO LEAVE IN 1952. BUSINESS HAD A GRAND OPENING IN JUNE 22, 1912 . IT CONSISTED OF A GENERAL STORE, POST OFFICE, A 3 STORY HOTEL, BOWLING ALLEY, TIN SHOP AND BAKERY. THE HOTEL HAD AUTOMATIC FIRE SPRINKLERS. THERE WAS A NATATORIUM WITH A POOL 50 X 160FT. THERE WERE 4 MILES OF PAVEMENT. CITY LIGHTS & WATER, TELEPHONE SYSTEM AND A NARROW GAUGE RAILROAD. BY 1914, 600 BUIDLING LOTS HAD BEEN SOLD AND 2000 PEOPLE INVOLVED. DUE TO EROSION CUTTING THE BANKS, THE NATATORIUM WAS DESTROYED IN 1932. OVER 20 HOMES HAD FALLEN INTO THE SEA BY 1949. IN 1952 THE SEA CUT A HALF MILE SWATH MAKING BAY OCEAN AN ISLAND. BREAKWATER WAS BUILT IN 1956 AND RE-ESTABLISHED THE PENINSULA. OF 59 HOMES AND SUMMER COTTAGES, ONLY 5 WERE MOVED IN TIME. ON FEB. 15, 1960 THE LAST HOUSE WASHED INTO THE SEA, AND THE CITY OF BAY OCEAN WAS BUT A DREAM AGAIN.

Signs not telling the whole story of Bayocean.

86'd is Forever

To my left at the long, lacquered, parquet bar of the Timeout Tavern on Highway 101 in downtown Tillamook lean three men. They all wear the bowling shirt-style uniform of a local automotive industry business. They're sodden at 6:00 pm on a weekday. No doubt they own the three bicycles parked out front, unlocked. Bicycles in front of any coastal tavern indicate good citizens—drinkers without driver's licenses and insurance are forgoing the wheel for handlebars.

"We started at breakfast," says the bearded one, apparently to no one in particular. He remains at the bar and orders another can of cheap Pacific Northwest lager of a brand formerly brewed in the Pacific Northwest. His buddy peels off to lose at video poker and support state services. The other man sways. He likely knows falling down means being 86'd. He likely also knows falling down means permanent exile from the Timeout since a sign over the bar reads, "86'd is forever."

It's festive here—in a corporate shilling sort of way. Busty babe promos for piss beers, mobiles for gimmick malt-based drinks, and placards exalting dead or alive NASCAR heroes decorate almost every available wall and ceiling space. It all brings to mind a line from a Nabokov short story titled, "The Fight": "The tavern was of the usual type—a couple of posters advertising drinks, some deer antlers, and a low, dark ceiling festooned with paper flaglets, remnants of some festival or other."

No antlers hang in the Timeout and the place is refreshingly light for an Oregon Coast tavern, but Nabokov pretty much nails it. Munich. Moscow. Tillamook. It's all really the same when it comes to a place where people congregate to drink beer and get drunk.

Suddenly the Timeout's door swings open and in walks a bearded, suspendered man with a KFC box under his left arm. In his right hand is a drumstick and he shreds it like a hyena on a downed wildebeest. There's a roar in the joint when the regulars notice the man. Everyone slams it into fifth gear for the upcoming malt-slicked straightaway that finally dead-ends when the tavern closes.

I take all this in from the Timeout as I sit at the bar facing north and consider recent Oregon Coast history. About ten miles west is Bayocean Spit. Two blocks east the Tillamook County Commissioners convene to rule on local land-use matters, including what type of development returns to Bayocean Spit, a stretch of sand that forms the precarious western edge of Tillamook Bay all the way to the Tillamook bar. I say "returns" because once there was considerable development out on the spit. It was called Bayocean Park and its impresario claimed it would be the "Atlantic City of the West." There was a hotel, a natatorium, a post office, a school, a newspaper called *The Surf*, vacation homes, hell maybe even a tavern. In 1912 there was a Grand Opening complete with a brass band and fireworks.

It's all gone now. It took about a score. It all slid into the sea because the planet obeyed physical laws. Waves make sand move. Buildings on moving sand collapse. The last home on Bayocean Spit got swallowed in 1960. There's a black-on-white billboard at the south entrance of the spit recounting the drama in shades of gray. It doesn't instruct.

Now schemes are afoot to develop Bayocean Spit again. That the spit isn't already a state park seized under the power of eminent domain is a failure on every conceivable level of Oregon representative government. But Bayocean Spit isn't a state park and multiple landowners, including Tillamook County, have recently commenced drooling over another go at Bayocean Spit. Preliminary ideas discussed include vacation homes, a paved road to the end, and, naturally, the rural economic panacea known as a golf course. Nothing can be ruled out, this being Tillamook County, so plans for a go-cart track, jail, dump or amphitheater for Air Supply or Kenny G to perform might be in the works.

Whatever madness is proposed, Tillamook County Commissioners will most likely weigh in on whether it all goes down, meaning whether or not concrete gets poured into footings on a dune. For those unacquainted with the current majority makeup of the board, all you need to know is they prove the American political maxim that the only public groups left in the nation where you get to be dumb, an asshole, lick the boots of your cronies, spend taxpayers' money, and get paid by taxpayers, are—rural county commissioners and big-time coaches at major universities.

As I said, I'm in the Timeout and the pace to the heart of darkness is getting rammed into full speed.

Still, given the opportunity by a wave of my wand, I believe a majority of the three bicycle owners would make a wiser decision about any proposed redevelopment of Bayocean Spit than Tillamook County Commissioners. It's not even close.

Before ruling, the Timeout board would need to sober up. Then they have to read three books.

The first is *Maimed by the Sea: Erosion Along the Coasts of Oregon and Washington—A Documentary* by Bert and Margie Webber. Published in 1983, this charming yet bracing study devotes most of its pages to the Bayocean debacle. ("An attack by Old King Neptune" is how the Webbers describe what happened.) The photographs and drawings are superb and shocking and one would think *Maimed by the Sea* should be legally required reading for any prospective coastal homebuyer, developer or coastal county commissioner.

It's simply astounding how many suckers Bayocean's impresario duped into an ecological fraud that went well beyond hubris. It was willful insanity. Of course if you study the history of vacation-home developments on Oregon's coastline, then you know this state has a disproportionate share of suckers when it comes to craving a home with a close-up ocean view—including former Oregon Governor and US Senator Mark Hatfield.

The second book is Paul D. Komar's concise and scholarly *The Pacific Northwest Coast: Living with the Shores of Oregon and Washington.* In this definitive account, he documents the inevitable history of inevitable erosion on Oregon's beaches. It's all there: Bayocean (1930-40s), Jump-Off Joe in Newport (1942 *and* early 1980s), Gleneden Beach (1965-71), Siletz Spit (1972-73), Nestucca Spit (1978), Alsea Spit (1982-83), and other Oregon Coast beach areas ad nauseam.

Komar's book came out in 1998 or otherwise he could have added Cape Lookout State Park in Netarts, The Capes development fiasco in Oceanside, and Oregon Governor John Kitzhaber's riprapped vacation home in Neskowin. Yes, Oregon's chief executive riprapped his beachfront vacation home. It was legal and it was surely the nadir for the office on the subject of the state's chief executive practicing ecology on his private property.

The Timeout board orders another round of cans. Even

55

in their current drunken state, even without reading the first two books, I still would prefer their majority decision right now over a majority decision by the Tillamook County Commissioners on a plan to redevelop Bayocean Spit. I sense the Timeout board would see the folly. Rural Americans aren't dumb. They possess wisdom and can receive wisdom.

Speaking of wisdom, there's a heaping portion of it offered in the last book the Timeout board must read, the New Testament. They don't need to read the whole thing, or even a chapter, just one paragraph, the last paragraph of Jesus' Sermon on the Mount, (Matthew 7:24-27):

Every one then who hears these words of mine and does them will be like a wise man who built his house upon the rock; and the rain fell, and the floods came, and the winds blew and beat upon that house, but it did not fall, because it had been founded on the rock. And every one who hears these words of mine and does not do them will be like a foolish man who built his house upon the sand; and the rain fell, and the floods came, and the winds blew and beat against that house, and it fell and great was the fall of it.

The WPA American Guide to Oregon.

The Straightening

*It may be regrettable to see this peaceful beautiful land trans-
formed into a network of highways, clogged with cars and
defaced with hot dog stands, the groves littered with tin cans
and papers, the hills pock-marked with stumps, and the cities
cursed with the slums that seem to accompany industrial
progress.*

Oregon: End of the Trail, American Guide Series (published
1940)

W e live with Speed and the need for the Instant.
Forget Walt Whitman's invitation to loaf and
invite your soul. It must be Fast and Now or it's

Uncool.

I reject this like I reject Internet access for my refrigerator or downloading instantaneous advice on backpacking Europe from roving, wired reporters.

Travel guides in print are fine. They induce a slower pace than digital communication, suggest deliberation, and are frequently outdated so a traveler has to adjust, pass little tests if Chernobyl exploded, the Berlin Wall got razed or the Aral Sea vanished.

I like that. I want a challenge for my mind and heart and the cool gadgetry creating Speed and the Instant murders any opportunity for both. That's why, when I travel the Oregon Coast, I use a 63-year old guide.

The Book

It was easy to write about Oregon. The state has something that inspires not provincial patriotism but affection.

The book, *Oregon: End of the Trail*, appearing in 1940, is part of a larger unprecedented story of perhaps the most fascinating publishing project in American history.

Compiled by an army of unaccredited authors, *Oregon: End of the Trail*, was just one of 48 state and three city guidebooks produced by the Federal Writers' Project of the Works Progress Administration (WPA), one of President Roosevelt's New Deal agencies.

The idea was to put unemployed writers to work by

visiting virtually every inhabited place in the country, document its heritage, and then shape the facts and anecdotes into an indispensable travel guide. These were no mere guidebooks cranked out by hacks, however. Studs Terkel, Ralph Ellison, Richard Wright and Saul Bellow were just some of the new talents enlisted to produce the books.

Even when originally published six decades ago, the guides were instantly recognized to have serious literary and historical merit because of their scope and superior writing. They took the brave editorial line of encouraging Depression-era Americans to hit the road, see their country, and pump discretionary spending into the sick economy. Now the books, collectively known as the *American Guide Series,* are regarded as classics in American non-fiction writing.

On the jacket cover, a blurb declares *Oregon: End of the Trail,* "Presents the story of past and present in panoramic style." It cost $2.50 when initially sold, an astonishing value even then considering the book is over 500 pages, contains photos and many maps, including a color, two-sided fold-out stored ingeniously in a back pocket.

The book begins with a precise overview of Oregon history (natural and political), culture, economy and demographics. The second section features major cities and part three, titled "All Over Oregon," profiles almost 40 "automobile tours."

The Tour

The automobile tours outlined in detail with all the accuracy humanly possible, unfolds to resident and visitor alike that part of the state not immediately visible to the casual observer

It's Tour 3 in the Guide that has led me down the old Oregon Coast three times. The Guide described the region as a series of "villages reeking with the smell of salmon oil." Back then, Oregon didn't even have a million residents and Bonneville Dam had just come on line. Portland was segregated. A few wolves still roamed the Cascades.

The route, from Astoria to Brookings, leisurely followed Highway 101, or the Roosevelt Military Highway as it was originally called. Construction on this meandering two-lane road began in 1921. When completed in 1932, it finally enabled travelers to drive all the way down the Oregon Coast. "It was only then," the Guide reports, "that along the coast real development began. Their long isolation has given the sea-board towns a certain individuality..."

According to the Guide, Highway 101 followed in part an old Indian trail and thus didn't afford all the postcard views that later the Oregon Highway Commission craved for tourists. Old Highway 101 transported people during the Depression but not very fast. And it winded a lot.

Clatsop County

Astoria is where Tour 3 starts and before the term multi-cultural was coined, the Guide describes the city as a place that, "never lacks the characteristics of the sea that has drawn Finns, Norwegians and Swedes in such numbers that shop signs in the various languages are commonplace."

In 1920 Astoria was the second most populated town in Oregon behind Portland. The salmon canning industry thrived but a devastating 1922 fire dispersed many people and the city never recovered its former glory.

Section A of Tour 3 begins across the rustic two-lane drawbridge over Young's River in East Astoria with Saddle Mountain presiding in the background. It's not quite as convenient as the zooming modern span (opened in 1965) that crosses the bay farther west and is the present-day route of Highway 101, but the old bridge is charmed with considerably more character and no one expects a driver to hurry over it. That's good, because the deliberate pace in this area provides the traveler a superb opportunity to check out all the clearcuts on private land.

These aren't your typical Coast Range clearcuts executed with utter malice toward coastal watersheds. According to an Associated Press report, an employee of a timber corporation has invented "designer clearcuts," which entails using computer modeling to aesthetically ameliorate what a piece of forested ground will look like after its been leveled. The employee does this by, "altering straight lines, feathering harsh edges and creating clumps of trees..." Apparently this makes the clearcuts look better from key vantage points in *nearby cities.*

After the Guide crosses Young's River, it digresses for several pages about the famed Lewis and Clark Expedition and quotes liberally from the journals. One entry details the "meager" first American Christmas in the Pacific Northwest in the winter of 1805 and another passage recounts how Lewis and Clark had to ban unruly Clatsop Indians from their fort after sunset.

The Guide reports at length about Lewis and Clark but it doesn't come across as a big deal, unlike the bicentennial commemoration, now officially underway. One aspect of the commemoration connected to the Oregon Coast is something called the Confluence Project, which calls for a series of sculptures designed by superstar architect Maya Lin to be erected at several river confluences traversed by Lewis and Clark. One of the confluences chosen is where the Columbia River meets the Pacific Ocean. This is a curious ecological selection considering how unnatural this confluence is today because of all the dikes, dams and dredging in the Columbia River Watershed.

A few miles south of Fort Clatsop, Highway 101 rolls through a now defunct town called Delmoor. Delmoor used to host an annual May festival that celebrated the seasonal bloom of Scotch broom, a plant "imported from Scotland for use in broom making and later used to bind the drifting sands of Clatsop Plains." Now the plant is classified as a noxious weed and convict crews all along the Oregon Coast labor to eradicate it.

Twenty miles from Astoria, the tour passes through Seaside, "Oregon's largest seaside resort, which spreads across the Necanicum River." Today this waterway, which qualifies for the state's "water quality limited" list because of excessive bacteria, is riprapped within the city limits and barely visible from the highway because of commercial development. What is visible here is a factory outlet mall.

At the Cannon Beach Junction south of Seaside, which now is the slabbed, intimidating intersection of Highway 101 and Highway 26, the tour heads inland for a few miles until it links with the present day Necanicum Highway (Highway 53). This curvy southern route enters Tillamook County near Mohler. Ironically, almost as soon as *Oregon: End of the Trail* was published, Highway 101 was reconfigured to course straight down the shore through a tunnel blasted through Arch Cape and a roadway hewn from Neahkahnie Mountain. This "improvement" marked the first of many to tear up the landscape and reroute the Oregon Coast Highway to afford better views and speed the trip.

Tillamook County

When the Guide's writer drove Tour 3 in the late 1930s, he took Highway 101 around Arch Cape and Neahkahnie Mountain through a valley. Here he describes loggers clearly visible from the road trimming and topping 200-foot trees with bare slopes "denuded" of forest in the background. The word "clearcut" wasn't part of the vocabulary then, but back in 2001 the Oregon Department of Forestry's "stewardship" allowed the thinning of naturally seeded, old trees in this area, called God's Valley, in order to "enhance wildlife habitat."

As the route reaches Mohler a bit farther down the road, the Guide counts another of the many yellow cheese factories in the county and how, "Many people of Swiss birth or descent operate dairies in the vicinity. They are particularly fond of playing the accordion and yodeling during the their leisure hours."

A few miles south of Mohler as the route skirts Nehalem Bay, the Guide notes the three fish packing houses nearby. They're all gone.

From Nehalem Bay, Tour 3 continues farther south into the heart of Tillamook County's dairy country, called Little Holland by the locals in the 1930s because of the many diked estuaries that created pastures for milk cows. Native Americans called Tillamook the "land of many waters."

Five rivers feed into Tillamook Bay and once they combined to create one of the most productive ecosystems in the world. As the Guide reports, "...just west of the Kilchis River Bridge is frequently inundated during winter rains. It is said that during these floods some motorists find salmon on their running boards." Now the Tillamook Bay Watershed suffers from high fecal bacteria levels, elevated water temperature, increased sediment loads from steep-slope logging in the Tillamook State Forest, loss of wetlands, paved-over floodplains, and illegal culverts and archaic tide gates that block anadromous fish passage. To make matters worse, just south of Garibaldi, Highway 101 was relocated straight through a section of the bay's tidal flats. The cumulative result is the ongoing death of wild salmonids and desperate local politics to save local pork barrel salmon hatcheries. Tillamook Bay also happens to be closed a third of the year to shellfish harvest, and it's not because of scarcity. Try manure run-off.

In the 1930s and 1940s, heading south from the city of Tillamook for 20 miles, the highway was a slow, narrow, windy, inland route. It's even more gloriously slow today behind 40-foot RVs pulling eight-cylinder vehicles. This section pretty much remains the same today as it did during Roosevelt's presidency, but not without a battle. In the 1960s, the imperious State Highway Commission led by Glenn Jackson wanted to move Highway 101 closer to the beach, straighten it, pave through dairy pastures, permanently split Pacific City, drive pilings into Nestucca Spit, and build a bridge over the entrance to Nestucca Bay. Oregon State Treasurer Bob Straub killed the plan.

Passing through a filled section of Nestucca Bay, Highway 101 rolls straight into Neskowin, a place name that means "plenty fish" in the local Native American language. The Guide enthuses about the area's "numerous varieties of fish," including the "silverside salmon," a term once used for Coho, a species now officially listed as "threatened" in Oregon Coast watersheds under the authority of the Endangered Species Act.

There's nothing written, however, about a mediocre

golf course built in the 1920s from a drained section of Neskowin Marsh. There's also no mention of, because they came later, a flat-roofed motel on a filled estuary that used to be a Native American archeological site, and a sewage treatment plant armored with riprap in floodplain. Nor quite obviously, could the Guide report that 60 years after its publication, certain affluent Neskowin "residents" blocked a potential acquisition of the golf course by the US Fish and Wildlife Service. It was an acquisition absolutely critical to improving fish habitat and passage.

In 1965, a new alignment of Highway 101 pushed over Cascade Head, instead of around it, at the southern end of Tillamook County. In the 1940s, the Guide's writer had to take the present-day Slab Creek Road east around Cascade Head, crossing into Lincoln County by way of Otis. Taking this 10-mile detour, which winds and car-sickening winds through an "experimental" forest (meaning it hasn't been clearcut in the last century) is one of the best ways to recreate the old Highway 101 automobile journey. Of course, a traveler does need about a half hour of extra time and a barf bag for the kids.

Lincoln County

According to the Guide, the north end of Lincoln County used to be a series of quaint towns distinguished by cottages, Japanese float decorations, and the proximity to Devil's Lake, which the "Indians believed that in these waters lived a monster that occasionally rose to the surface to attack men."

But something was lost in the legend's translation because the monster in North Lincoln County came not to attack men, but the landscape, ecology, Native American sovereignty and the Caucasian inhabitants' sense of beauty.

Today, Devil's Lake is officially listed as "water quality limited" for excessive pH and chlorophyll a levels and has virtually no native vegetation because thousands of grass carp were dumped there in the 1980s and 1990s to control non-native plants.

This area should be part of a massive 1.4 million acre coastal Indian reservation, established in 1855, but closed in 1925 after the disaster of allotment. Later the Siletz tribe, indigenous to the Lincoln County area, was "terminated," then "restored" in 1977 by an act of Congress. Now there's hardly any Siletz land at all near the Oregon Coast, except for the Chinook Winds Casino in Lincoln City. What dominates here is motels, fast food restaurants, cheap construction, gas stations, gift shops, pawn shops, car lots and all other examples of commercial blight championed by "the boosting activities of chambers of commerce," a prescient warning issued by the Guide.

Former Oregon Governor Mark Hatfield once described this section of Highway 101 as the "20 miserable miles," mocking a chamber of commerce slogan. Another governor, Tom McCall, threatened to have the state take over Lincoln County's land use planning because local efforts in the early 1970s were an aesthetic embarrassment and environmental disaster that led to outrages like raw sewage flowing out to the beach. "Lincoln City was a model of strip city grotesque," McCall wrote in his autobiography.

Leaving present-day Lincoln City, Highway 101 once cruised awkwardly into Kernville and over the Siletz River on a tight bridge. The road continued on narrow strip of elevated land through Siletz Bay's tidal marsh, filled long ago by enterprising Pioneers in an act of unmitigated disaster for an estuary. Later a bigger, straighter, four-lane bridge across the Siletz River was constructed and more material dumped in the estuary to accommodate the expansion. Highway 101 in Oregon is called the Oregon Coast Highway, but with the fill dumped into Siletz, Nestucca, Tillamook, Nehalem, and other bays, ad nauseam, it might as well be called the Oregon Coast Filled-Estuary Highway.

The highway improvement through Siletz Bay, though, is especially egregious. When coupled with the presence of the Salishan Resort development, its golf course and homes out on the riprapped dunes of Siletz Spit, the result is what one veteran Oregon coastal planner described as, "positively the worst ecological and aesthetic development on the Oregon Coast." But it could have been even worse. In the late 1960s there were plans to fill more sections of the bay to construct an airport and vacation homes. Today a few people want to dredge it for water-skiing.

Continuing down Highway 101, the Guide approaches Depoe Bay, now the sight of a massive condo complex called The Resort at Whale Pointe (sic), a World Mark Resort, part

68

of Trendwest's empire of garish leisure. Tom McCall once coined a phrase to describe what's happened to Depoe Bay in recent years--"coastal condomania." Whale Pointe is a development that obliterates any non-member's opportunity to see the ocean from here, much less the famous migrating whales. The gentrification also assures that a gritty fishing boat scene like the one filmed here in *One Flew over the Cuckoo's Nest* will never happen again.

South of Depoe Bay, a curious sign promoting a gated community advertises a "private beach," which is supposed to be illegal in Oregon. Someone must have found yet another loophole in Oregon's overrated land use protection laws and bulldozed through there in the name of 'private property rights,' a phrase never once appearing in the 549-page Guide.

A few miles from Depoe Bay is a place ironically known as Otter Crest. Otter Rock looms offshore. The Guide reports, "Sea otters, long prized for their glossy fur, formerly abounded in these waters." They're all gone, extirpated in Oregon waters, the subject of expensive reintroduction efforts that all failed.

It's near Otter Rock that Highway 101 was improved from the curvy, slow, lean road along the shore (called Otter Crest Loop today). Engineers chose a straighter, fatter route over a slide-prone headland area to the east. Practically every winter since the improvement, the vexed Oregon Department of Transportation has provided full employment for local construction workers.

The tour rolls into Newport, where according to the

Guide, the US Army wanted to build a fort in 1856, but the best spot happened to be covered by hundreds of Native American burial canoes. As the story goes, "After mediation the Indians suddenly agreed to the removal of the canoes, but refused to take them away themselves." The Army solved the problem by launching the canoes at high tide out to sea, forever separating them from their spiritual resting place.

Perhaps multiple episodes of cosmic tribal revenge were exacted for this desecration many years later at Jump-Off Joe, a rock named for a local Native American near Newport's Nye Beach, "...from which, legend says," the Guide reports, "the usual maiden and her lover flung themselves." In 1942, a nearby landslide flung more than a dozen houses into the surf. Then in the early 1980s the same disaster nearly struck an unfinished controversial condo development in the same slide-prone area. It was ordered razed by the same local authorities who approved it.

In Newport, the Guide also notes, "The view of the (Yaquina) Bay at sunset, when the fishing fleet rides at anchor, is particularly attractive."

The sunsets still look good, but the fishing fleet has fallen on hard times. Salmon are scarce and the groundfish stocks have nearly been wiped out, leading to new catch restrictions, an economic emergency declaration, federal disaster funds, and welfare programs modeled on the same New Deal policy, relief, that started the Federal Writers' Project and built state parks all down the Oregon Coast.

Section B of Tour 3 begins south of Newport. The

70

Guide describes Waldport as a place where "its inhabitants still make a living by clam and crab fishing and packing, though summer visitors are an increasingly important source of income."

It's hard to imagine today how any Waldport resident makes a living from the sea. But those "summer visitors" did increase. Just look to the vacation homes crammed together on the sand of Alsea Spit. They weren't there in 1940. They weren't even there when Ken Kesey wrote about this wild wet place in *Sometimes a Great Notion* in the early 1960s.

Lane County

Entering Lane County just past Yachats, the Guide describes how Highway 101 parallels the beach and relates a story about a crafty "hobo" who made a perfect three-part weld at a blacksmith shop stunning the locals. The brief narrative also employs the term "tramp" to define what we would now call a "homeless" person. During the Depression there must have been many "hobos" and "tramps" with bindles hitchhiking Highway 101, looking or not looking for work. Homeless men still hitchhike Highway 101. No bindles in this afflent era. Backbacks now.

Many things have changed near Highway 101 in over half a century since the Guide waxed so wonderfully about the Oregon Coast, but one of the constants is the Sea Lion Caves, an attraction the Guide explains in a sexy and enthusiastic summary. The tourists loved the sea lions and the seals in the era of the *American Guide,* but many coastal locals and

Oregon fish and game officials loathed them, claiming the pinnipeds ate too many salmon.

So the fishermen shot them with impunity; the state sponsored a bounty program and pinnipeds off the Oregon Coast nearly went the way of old growth trees—wiped out. Only the 1972 Marine Mammal Protection Act (MMPA), signed by President Richard Nixon, which made it a federal crime to kill pinnipeds, saved seals and sea lions from extirpation in West Coast coastal waters. Now that the seal and sea lion numbers have dramatically rebounded, angry talk that they eat too many salmon (hatchery-bred this time around) has returned. A few folks walk their talk and every year a few Oregon Coast pinnipeds have their heads blown with total impunity because the MMPA is barely enforced. Currently, Congress is being lobbied hard to amend the law to allow fishermen to shoot "nuisance" pinnipeds.

Continuing south from the Sea Lion Caves, the journey comes to Florence. In this section the Guide barely mentions the miles of sand dunes that today comprise the Oregon Dunes National Recreation Area and are home to a lively and loud off road vehicle scene that certainly would have appalled the Guide's writers. They valued the state's beauty on a simple visceral level and would've never conceived that just being in Oregon's unique natural spaces wasn't satisfying enough. They didn't need toys.

Back in the 1950s, US Senator Richard Neuberger tried to persuade the National Park Service to declare the dunes around Florence a National Seashore Park. A few locals raised considerable opposition, came together to incorporate a town called Dunes City, and successfully thwarted the designation. Locals stopped the park idea then, but in 1972 the dunes became a National Recreation Area, which allows for considerably more development, off road vehicles and "hot-dog stands."

Into Gardiner the tour continues. The Guide reports why most of the structures in town were white, apparently the obsession of a young manager of the lumber mill. Today the buildings aren't all white. The sprawling, rusted timber mill looks deserted. The mill manager is gone. Other humans with a very different obsession have replaced him.

In 2000, a New Age non-profit religious corporation called Living Love Fellowship relocated to Gardiner and moved into the former headquarters of International Paper. They refer to themselves as Amadonians. In addition to selling liquor license consulting services, they believe in extraterrestrials and follow the teachings from a bible written by space aliens.

Douglas County

Crossing the Umpqua River near an island where Native Americans ambushed a party headed by Jedediah Smith, killed 18 men, and made off with $20,000 in pelts, Highway 101 rolls into Reedsport. Today the island is an abandoned industrial site and literally rusts while waiting on the market for redevelopment. It seems Reedsport has a history of civic blight because the Guide provides the town with the most unflattering description of any place on the Oregon Coast. "Much of Reedsport was filled in from earth cut from the sandy clay banks of the hills behind the town. Most of the population lives in the dozen or so two-story rooming houses and hotels and is composed of transient laborers. South of Reedsport Highway 101 climbs through denuded hills where stumps and blackened snags are evidence of the death of the local lumber industry."

New clearcuts in exactly the same area are visible today.

Coos County

The route crosses over the narrow, arched Coos Bay Bridge, into North Bend and serious timber country. Or what used to be serious timber country. Although the nearby hills above Coos Bay are clearcut in the usual steep-slope rapine manner, all the big trees are gone and now many log trucks rattling down Highway 101 carry "pecker poles."

"Marshfield (now called Coos Bay) is near the top of the crooked arm of Coos Bay, which is usually crowded with schooners being loaded with lumber cut in the forests of the Coast Range," the Guide reports. This place used to thrive and the miles of docks along Coos Bay surely bustled. Today they're forlorn, deserted and seemingly ready for a Superfund listing. Perhaps the one piece of good news about the docks came a few years ago when the Coquille tribe built a casino there, called it The Mill, and named the lounge the Hook Tender Saloon.

Leaving Coos Bay, the tour heads southeast toward Coquille and then west to Bandon to reconnect with the shore. Today this route is State Highway 42. In the late 1950s when the highway straighteners wanted to route Highway 101 directly to Bandon bypassing Coquille, the locals raised hell. As in most cases, the Highway Commission won and everyone else lost, except for those who didn't mind if the state cut trees, drained wetlands, and paved more land so tourists could shave a few minutes off a trip and bypass a working-class town.

Crossing the Coquille River into Bandon on the contemporary Highway 101 route provides beautiful views of the estuary and ocean. But below the bridge, the river reveals the cost of development and material progress: much of the Coquille Basin's water is either too hot for fish, too full of bacteria, or has elevated dissolved oxygen levels. About 1940s Coquille the Guide boasts, "Within the city limits it is possible to fish for several varieties of salmon, steelhead, and trout." By 2003, some of these species have vanished from many coastal tributaries and local subsidized farmers quote anti-private property passages from the *Communist Manifesto* at public meetings and say they are living under a "totalitarian" regime because the state wants them to quit polluting public watercourses.

The Guide describes Bandon as "a resort with a beach at the mouth of the Coquille River," and claims it "was known as the most beautiful town in southern Oregon," until a forest fire blew in from the east and "wiped it out." Bandon was under reconstruction when the WPA writer visited. Today it's a smart-looking city with a reputation for somewhat pretentious attitudes (some boosters now call it Bandon by the Sea) and the site of a newly constructed links golf course where the affluent jet in from all over the country to play. This venture has proved so successful that other coastal areas' politicians and Babbitts desperate to create more tourist opportunities for rich people have showcased Bandon Dunes Golf Course as the best new way to exploit the landscape near the ocean.

According to the Guide, Bandon was named after the hometown of an Irish peer who settled there and imported Irish furze, a plant, "that in early spring yellows the sand hills along the highway southward; a thorny shrub, its pea-like flowers have an odor similar to that of coconut oil." Furze, or gorse, as it's better known, has now become an ecological vandal to the point that vacant lots are considered more valuable if they're gorse-free. Presently, gorse is confined to the Southern Oregon Coast. It's slowly invading north, up Highway 101.

Today a few miles south of Bandon there's another example of exotic species tainting the landscape. It's called West Coast Game Park and this attraction features 21 acres of confined animals, including leopards, black panthers and tigers.

South of Bandon to the California is obviously different than circa 1940, but this most inaccessible part of the Oregon Coast most resembles what the WPA writers saw.

76

They wrote little about this stretch, perhaps hoping people would ignore it.

Curry County

The Guide calls Curry County the "most primitive county in Oregon and long isolated by lack of roads." Only around 1000 people lived in the county in 1940 according to the Guide's numbers. It's still tough to reach and there's considerably less development here than anywhere else near Highway 101. In the 1960s the straighteners came through anyway and literally paved the way for the last great surge of county commission-approved rapine on the Oregon Coast. It hasn't happened—yet.

Just north of Port Orford, the tour passes through Sixes, "on the banks of a small river of the same name noted for its steelhead," an anadromous fish species that spawns in small tributaries high up in the watersheds and is disappearing on the Southern Oregon Coast.

West of Highway 101 is Cape Blanco, named by Spanish mariners in 1603 and allegedly the first spot in Oregon seen (claimed) by Europeans. Over 350 years later, in 1971, it became a state park with overnight camping amenities, a development that didn't occur again on the Oregon Coast until Whalen Island in Tillamook County was established in 2000.

Into Port Orford, famous for its type of cedar, where the Guide maintains Jack London once briefly stayed and was reputed to have written part of *The Valley of the Moon*.

"South of Port Orford the mountains press close to

the sea and the highway curves along a shelf high above the waves," the Guide reports. Finally at the summit the route briefly leveled and then steeply descended to the mouth of a canyon. It has been said by many who traveled it, that this part of the tour was the most spectacular, slow, turning, tight, bending, windswept, unique, thrilling, rugged and gorgeous stretch of the entire old Oregon Coast Highway. It took time, patience and skill to drive, but it rewarded.

This slow way is gone, now part of a three-mile hiking trail in Humbug Mountain State Park. Realignment in the 1960s straightened the highway, brought it down from the hills, practically on the beach, along a creek, and today its widened lanes speed the motorist along. At the top of the trail there's a picnic table on the exact spot that must have been the most dreaded hairpin turn on the entire old Oregon Coast Highway. A visitor can eat lunch here, look 1000 feet down to the new stretch of Highway 101, see vehicles hurtling by in a blur, then turn around to take in the two-lane wonder of the old route now nearly overcome with brush.

About 30 miles south of Port Orford is where the Rogue River enters the Pacific and Gold Beach greets visitors. "The Rogue is famous for steelhead and salmon fishing," the Guide boasts. The river still has that reputation although hatchery releases here and in practically every basin on the Oregon Coast were (and are) necessary to keep the sports fishing industry alive and deflect concerns that wild fish numbers are a fraction of what they used to be in every coastal basin.

As for the town of Gold Beach, according to the Guide, a saloon in the town once doubled as the county's courthouse and "gold was passed freely across the counter." It's not that exciting today, but there's big money in trophy homes to be made in this area.

Recently though, someone monkey-wrenched part of the impending development in the Gold Beach vicinity by selling 258 acres of scenic property at Cape Sebastian to the state, which plans to roll the land into the existing Cape Sebastian State Park.

Heading south to the California border and the Guide offers only a few paragraphs about the history of the area (a massacre of Indians by vigilantes at the mouth of the Pistol River) and nothing about contrived tourist attractions. There weren't such contrivances on this stretch of the Oregon Coast during the Depression. There were only gorgeous natural features.

During the *American Guide* heyday, near the Pistol River, Highway 101 used to head away from the beach, leisurely into the mountains to Carpenterville. Twenty miles later a driver ended up in Brookings. The Guide describes the summit near Carpenterville as "the highest point of the highway," (elevation 1,715). On clear days a visitor can find Mt. Shasta to the southeast. Scanning west is to take in the Pacific Ocean as far as weather permits. Sixty years ago, looking down from Carpenterville towards the beach, there was no river of highway.

This is the finest view on the Oregon Coast, truly

awesome. One can envision the Guide's writer getting out of his car, marveling, taking notes, smoking a cigarette, anxious to begin pounding a typewriter to describe this unique Oregon and American scene. To recreate this experience from three score ago, a traveler must take the old Highway 101 route through Carpenterville. It takes 45 extra minutes.

The Carpenterville road is narrow, winding, bumpy, switchbacked, vertigo-inducing, tree-canopied and deer-choked. Rusted old Highway 101 guardrails still protect. In places, heading south, a driver can catch glimpses of the ocean—and the relocated Highway 101. In 1962, the road improvers prevailed again and pulled the route down from the hills. As a town, Carpenterville soon went away. It's still on some maps.

The new Highway 101 parallels the beach and bisects a pristine state park named for Samuel Boardman with acres and acres of asphalt. The way to Brookings is straight and fast.

Finally, Tour 3 concludes with a brief reference to Brookings, "grew up around a sawmill," and a mention that Crescent City, California is 21 miles from the border. The trip is over. Now read the multi-part question below posed by Guide's authors in the introduction:

Will the sons of the impending industrial age
be shorter and shrewder, and the daughters
dependent for their beauty upon commodities
sold in drug-stores; and will Oregonians be-

come less appreciative of nature and rooted living and more avid and neurotic in the pursuit of wealth?

I've driven Tour 3A four times now. I know the answers. Consider what William Blake wrote in *Proverbs of Hell* about a century before the automobile was invented:

Improvement makes straight roads; but the crooked roads without
    improvement are roads of Genius.

A 1977 booklet published by the State of Oregon.

One for One for One

Intrigued by a footnote in a monograph on the history of the Oregon state parks, I went to the Web to begin a search for the cited book.

It's called *Oregon's Beaches: A Birthright Preserved* written by Kathryn Straton and published in 1977 by Oregon State Parks and Recreation. I live at the Oregon Coast. I write about it as a passion and have read practically every book produced on the subject.

I had never seen or heard of this book prior to coming across the footnote.

I first went to Powells.com, the online outlet of the famous Portland bookstore. Naturally it would be there, Portland being in Oregon and Oregon famous for its open beaches.

Not one copy. Next I hit the Barnes and Noble site, which I had read is linked to hundreds if not thousands of rare book dealers across the country. One copy existed at Escape Fiction in Salem, Oregon. I ordered it at $6.95. I would have paid $50.

It was on its way in a few business days, but I couldn't wait. I drove immediately to the Pacific City branch of the Tillamook County Library and launched a search. Two copies in the system.

Two days later I received a call from the librarian ten minutes before closing. *Oregon Beaches: A Birthright Preserved* was in. I live 15 minutes from the library. I had the book in my possession in seven. I drove to a tavern and ordered a beer. I devoured the 77-page book before taking a sip.

It's an understatement to say I was overcome after reading this book. I thought I knew what had gone down to save Oregon's beaches. I had written plenty of articles about it. This book set me straight not unlike Paul's experience with a blinding light on the road to Damascus. Thus imbued, sitting there in a tavern not far from the beach, an idea, more like a demand, suddenly came to me. I call it "One for One for One."

In the book's foreword, Governor Bob Straub wrote: "(It)...reminds Oregonians that the public's long-established right to have access to and enjoy this exceptional resource was in grave doubt just a decade ago."

Straub kicks off *Oregon Beaches: A Birthright Preserved* in his typical rigorous style. He perfectly sets the table for the reader to discover, through Straton's expert documentation, how the "Beach Bill" (House Bill 1601) faced abortion in the Legislature and hung in precarious state constitutional balance for some time after its delivery. It was close. The usual cabals entered into their usual seedy alliances and wanted all Oregon sand above the high tide line for themselves and their cronies to desecrate with pavement, espresso carts, cabanas and fat security guards.

Can you imagine Oregon today with fenced-off, private beaches and condos on pilings down to the high tide line? With surveillance cameras and private parties? In fact, that the "Beach Bill" became a law, much less a national model for conservation, was a political miracle made only possible by a few dedicated Oregon gods who never gave up the faith in the rightness of open, publicly-owned Oregon beaches.

I doubt a current Oregon legislator could name any of them. It's also pretty telling when a representative from a national environmental group with an office in Portland comes down to the Oregon Coast and gets the year of the "Beach Bill" wrong in a presentation on protecting marine areas.

Kathryn Straton wrote *Oregon Beaches: A Birthright Preserved.* Who was (is) Kathryn Straton I wondered?

I finished my pint, drove home, went online, and Googled Ms. Straton. It kicked me back a phone number at the Oregon Department of Transportation. I called it. I heard the voice of an angel. We played phone tag for several days and then finally connected. She was happy to talk.

"It was my first and only book," said Straton, who was then working for the Historic Preservation Office of the

Oregon State Parks and Recreation Branch. As she recalled, back in 1977, ten years after the passage of the "Beach Bill," there was grave concern within her agency that Oregonians had forgotten the importance of the law and what it meant to public recreation.

"There was a sense of urgency to get something out on the record," Straton said. She was asked if she wanted the job. She had no literary background but accepted the challenge and produced a very, very important book for Oregon.

And what a book! *Oregon Beaches: A Birthright Preserved* contains a concise narrative of the events leading up to the "Beach Bill " and the sordid Republican machinations in the House that tried to kill the proposed law. The book recaps the fascinating but unsuccessful legal challenges to the law and as a bonus includes photographs, footnotes and a rich bibliography. About the only thing missing from *Oregon Beaches: A Birthright Preserved* is the behind-the-scenes story of the extraordinary public involvement that kept the "Beach Bill" alive. But that wasn't really Straton's editorial charge.

Of course today it's totally inconceivable that a bill with one atom of foresight such as the "Beach Bill" would pass the Oregon Legislature, much less be introduced. Moreover, any notion that a bill passed by a contemporary Oregon Legislature would be commemorated later with a book produced by a state agency at taxpayer expense is roughly equal to reversing a Newtonian law.

Straton remembered the initial and only press run of *Oregon Beaches: A Birthright Preserved* at about 500, but maybe 1000.

"It was distributed to libraries, state agencies and sold at state parks along the Oregon Coast," she said. The book wasn't available in bookstores. According to Straton, since its publication over 25 years ago, there have been discussions about reprinting the book with an update on the sleazy and never-ending counterattacks on the "Beach Bill." There was even talk about Governor Straub writing a new foreword.

Nothing ever came of the reprint idea and Governor Straub has sadly passed away. But the need for this book is greater than ever. The battle for the soul of the Oregon Coast is still raging. I would say presently the forces aligned with Beaches Forever Inc. are pretty much getting their collective ass kicked.

Just imagine today how an updated, utterly slick, re-printed, hyper-marketed *Oregon Beaches: A Birthright Preserved* could serve as a Tom Paine-like polemical weapon of destruction against the Grasping Wastrels.

And just imagine mailing the new book to every Oregon legislator and coastal county commissioner in a neat package that includes a vial of sand from Bob Straub State Park and the famous photograph of Governor McCall standing on Cannon Beach in front of the Surfsand Motel.

Obviously, the state formerly functioning as Oregon cannot help with the printing cost anytime soon, hence my idea (demand). I call it "One for One for One," as in one salary (including benefits) of one Portland-based environmental group staffer for one year. According to my estimate, that would just about cover the cost of resurrecting *Oregon Beaches: A Birthright Preserved* and put it in play again, but this time with much larger fanfare and "urgency" than in 1977. Now wouldn't this be a more meaningful way to spend precious conservation dollars than paying a green staffer to send email alerts, make losing wonky public comments, raising money for more green staffers, prettying the Web site, or preparing pretty GIS maps? Besides, it's only for one year and then the staffer can get back to work implementing political strategies that do practically nothing to protect Oregon's natural resources. These current strategies exist to employ urban people in energy efficient buildings.

"One for One for One" calls for a sacrifice. Perhaps there's an environmental group in Portland not drunk on institutional self-interest with a leader, who, once checking out *Oregon Beaches: A Birthright Preserved* from a library and reading it, will recognize that Kathryn Straton wrote a minor Oregon journalism classic over 25 years ago. Perhaps the book didn't matter then. It could matter now.

We need it now, pushed hard in the face of elected officials and citizens who don't know or respect the "Beach Bill" or this state's (once) unsurpassed legacy of preserving its beaches for *exclusive* public use. Straton's nearing retirement and told me she would gladly volunteer her impending free time to research and update the book. She knows what's at stake on the Oregon Coast the next few years. It's really the last battle left, and it's the same battle all over again. Is there an Oregon environmental group out there ready to take up her offer and do something magnificent with their donors' money? There's still a world of open Oregon Coast sand to win.

"Coastal condomania" in Depoe Bay blocking the public's view of the ocean.

Postcript

House bill would end barrier to using riprap on beaches

From *The Oregonian,* May 2, 2003.

Salem—The House pushed aside environmentalists' concern Thursday to pass a bill that would make it easier to use riprap on Oregon beaches.

House Bill 3228 would prevent the state Land Conservation and Development Commission from prohibiting the use of protective structures, such as riprap, around homes, businesses, bridges and other coastal projects built before 1977.

Rep. Alan Brown, R-Newport, sponsored the bill to avoid the review process...

...The bill, which passed 32-24, is expected to face opposition in the Senate.

Doing nothing useful on Nestucca Spit.

Bibliography

Books

Aikens, C., Melvin, *Archaeology of Oregon*, (Portland, US Department of the Interior, Bureau of Land Management, 1993)

Armstrong, H. Chester, *History of Oregon State Parks,* (Salem, Oregon State Parks, 1965)

American Guide Series—*Oregon: End of the Trail*, (Portland, Binford and Mort Publishers, 1940)

Boardman, S.H., *Oregon State Park System: A Brief History*, *Oregon Historical Quarterly*, (Volume LV, September 1954, Number 3)

Burbank, Luther, *Luther Burbank: His Methods and Discoveries and Their Practical Application*, Vol. VI, (New York, Luther Burbank Press, 1914)

Cone, Joseph, Ridlington, Sandy, eds., *The Northwest Salmon Crisis: A Documentary History*, (Corvallis, Oregon State University Press, 1996)

Coulton, Kevin G., Williams, Philip, B., Bener, Patricia, A., *An Environmental History of the Tillamook Bay Estuary and Watershed*, (Tillamook Bay National Estuary Project, 1996)

Cox, Thomas R., *The Park Builders: A History of State Parks in the Pacific Northwest* (Seattle, University of Washington Press, 1988)

Dicken, Samuel, N., Dicken, Emily, F., *The Making of Oregon: A Study in Historical Geography*, (Portland, Oregon Historical Society, 1979)

Dreyer, Peter, *Gardener Touched by Genius, The Life and Times of Luther Burbank* (University of California Press, 1985)

Gibbs, Jim, *Oregon's Salty Coast*, (Seattle, Superior Publishing Company, 1978)

Hayes, Derek, *Historical Atlas of the Pacific Northwest*, (Seattle, Sasquatch Books, 1999)

Jackson, Philip, Kimerling A. Jon, eds., *Atlas of the Pacific Northwest*, (Corvallis, Oregon State University Press, 1993)

Komar, Paul, D., *The Pacific Northwest Coast: Living with the Shores of Oregon and Washington*, (Durham, Duke University Press, 1998)

Lucia, Ellis, ed., *This Land Around Us: A Treasury of Pacific Northwest Writing*, (Garden City, New York, Doubleday & Company Inc., 1969)

Loy, William, G., *Atlas of Oregon*, (Eugene, University of Oregon Books, 1977)

Mackenzie, John P. S., *Birds in Peril: A guide to the endangered birds of the United States and Canada*, (Toronto, Pagurian Press, 1977)

McCall, Tom, with Neal, Steve, *Tom McCall: Maverick*, (Portland, Binford and Mort Publishers, 1977)

McCarthur, Lewis, A., McCarthur, Lewis, L., *Oregon Geographic Names*, (Portland, Oregon Historical Society, 1982)

Oregon Blue Book, (Salem, State Printing Office, many editions)

Pojar, Jim, MacKinnon, Andy, eds., *Plants of the Pacific Northwest Coast*, (Redmond, Lone Pine Publishing, 1994)

Rock, Alexandria, *Short History of the Little Nestucca River Valley and its early Pioneers*, (Tillamook County, 1947)

Sauter, John, Johnson, Bruce, *Tillamook Indians of the Oregon Coast*, (Portland, Binford and Mort Publishers, 1974)

Taylor III, Joseph, Evans, *A Persistent Calling: The Commercial Fishing History of Pacific City, Oregon*, (Honor's Thesis, University of Oregon, School of History, 1990)

Taylor III, Joseph, Evans, *Making Salmon: An Environmental History of the Northwest Fisheries Crisis*, (Seattle, University of Washington Press, 1999)

Straton, Kathryn, *Oregon's Beaches: A Birthright Preserved*, (Salem, Oregon Parks and Recreation Branch, 1977)

Tyler, Robert, L., *Rebels of the Woods; the IWW in the Pacific Northwest*, (Eugene, University of Oregon Books, 1967)

Webber, Bert and Margie, *Maimed by the Sea: Erosion Along the Coasts of Oregon and Washington—A Documentary*, (Fairfield, Washington, Ye Galleon Press, 1983)

Weisberger, Bernard, A., ed., *The WPA Guide to America*, (New York, Pantheon Books, 1985)

Williams, Henry, Smith, ed., *Luther Burbank: His Life and Work*, (New York, Hearst's International Library Co., 1915)

Walth, Brent, *Fire at Eden's Gate: Tom McCall and the Oregon Story*, (Portland, Oregon Historical Society, 1994)

Young, Carolyn, ed., *Oregon Environmental Atlas*, (Portland, Oregon Department of Environmental Quality, 1988)

Studies and Documents

A Citizen's Guide to the 4(d) Rule for Threatened Salmon and Steelhead on the West Coast, (National Marine Fisheries Service, 2000)
Crisis in Oregon Estuaries: A Summary of Environmental Factors Affecting Oregon Estuaries, (Corvallis, Oregon State University Marine Advisory Board, 1970)

Environmental Assessment: Proposed Nestucca Bay National Wildlife Refuge (Portland, US Fish and Wildlife Service, 1990)

Federal Register, Vol. 64, No. 148, Tuesday, August 3, 1999, Department of the Interior, Fish and Wildlife Service, *Endangered and Threatened Wildlife and Plants; Proposal To Remove the Aleutian Canada Goose From the List of Endangered and Threatened Wildlife.*

Natural Resources of Nestucca Estuary, (Portland, prepared by Richard M. Starr, Oregon Department of Fish and Wildlife, 1979)

Oregon and Offshore Oil, (Corvallis, Oregon State University Sea Grant College Program, 1978)

Oregon Estuary Plan Book, (Salem, Department of Land Conservation and Development, 1987)

Oregon Highway Park System, 1921-1989, An Administrative History (Salem, Oregon Parks and Recreation Department, 1992)

Oregon Plan for Salmon and Watersheds, (Salem, Office of the Governor, State of Oregon, 1999)

Review of 2000 Ocean Salmon Fisheries, (Portland, Pacific Fishery Management Council, 2001)

Tillamook Bay Task Force Report, (Oregon State University Extension Service, 1976)

TMDL and Water Quality Management Plan for the Tillamook Bay Watershed, (Portland, Oregon Department of Environmental Quality, 2001)

TMDL and Water Quality Management Plan for the Nestucca Bay Watershed, (Portland, Oregon Department of Environmental Quality, 2001)

303(d) List, (Portland, Oregon Department of Environmental Quality, 1999)

The author and Dr. Bob Bacon drinking martinis in the Sandtrap Lounge.

VISIT *the* **OREGON COAST** *highway* **U.S. 101**

IT'S AIR-CONDITIONED!

Top Left—In Depoe Bay
Top Right—Heceta Head
Lower Left—Humbug Park
Lower Right—Devil's Elbow

IN ALL THE WORLD
NO DRIVE LIKE THIS